D1587297

C015518810

1963

1963
That Was the Year That Was

Andrew Cook

In memory of my father
and the walk on Wardown Lake

First published 2013

The History Press
The Mill, Brimscombe Port
Stroud, Gloucestershire, GL5 2QG
www.thehistorypress.co.uk

British Library Cataloguing in Publication Data.
A catalogue record for this book is available from the British Library.

ISBN 978 0 7524 8724 3

Typesetting and origination by The History Press
Printed in Great Britain

CONTENTS

ACKNOWLEDGEMENTS

I would like to thank the following for their much appreciated assistance in the writing and production of this book: Bill Adams, Jordan Auslander (USA), Dmitry Belanovsky (Russia), Alia Cook, Edward Laxton, Gavin McGuffie, Hannah Renier, Lindsey Smith, Phil Tomaselli, Chris Williamson and the staff at the British Library Newspaper Collections.

INTRODUCTION

While we conveniently package the past into decades when talking about the 'Roaring '20s', 'the Rock and Roll era' of the '50s or the 'Swinging '60s', these tend to be labels of convenience rather than of historical accuracy.

In reality, the first four years of the 1950s were more akin to the 1940s, with austerity and rationing still facts of everyday life. Likewise, the first three years of the '60s were, in terms of fashion, social attitudes and living standards, really part of the 1950s. The year 1963 was to be the seminal year when most of the things we now associate with the 'Swinging '60s' really began.

The year 1963 was also the time of my earliest childhood recollection: during the coldest winter for nearly 300 years, my father took me to a lake not far from where we lived; it was completely frozen and we were able to walk across it; we stopped in the middle and my father told me I should never forget that moment as it was unlikely to ever happen again in my lifetime. I never have.

This year was also the year that satire entered the mainstream through a new ground-breaking TV series called *That Was The Week That Was*, and from where the idea for the title of this book came. The series lampooned the political and social Establishment of the day, targeting figures such as Prime Minister Harold Macmillan and Home Secretary Henry Brooke, who by 1963 seemed to personify a by-gone era. Other targets were the monarchy, the queen, Britain's declining status as a world power, racism, social hypocrisy and the British class system. Though broadcast well after my bedtime, it seemed that, along with The Beatles, it was to be an on-going topic of conversation between my teenage cousins, although I had no idea who or what they were talking about until many years later.

9

The concept of 1963 being the gateway to the 1960s and beyond was a theme I lectured on during my time at Birkbeck College, University of London during the mid-1980s. For American undergraduates, keen to understand the British political system and the colossal changes that have taken place since the 1950s, these events provided a ready-made introduction. Much of what follows in this book is taken from the research and lecture notes I wrote at the time. However, thirty years later, we now know a great deal more about 1963 than we did in 1983. I have, therefore, sought to update these chronicles by incorporating new information that has been released by a variety of institutions and archives, both in the UK and the US, during the interim period. This additional material is outlined in the bibliography and sources section at the end of the book.

Most years before and after 1963 have been fortunate to experience more than three or four seminal events during their allotted twelve months; a cursory look through a chronology of 1963, however, reminds us just how many significant events took place that year.

TIMELINE

JANUARY

- **14 January** – George C. Wallace becomes governor of Alabama. In his inaugural speech, he defiantly proclaimed, 'segregation now, segregation tomorrow, and segregation forever!'
- **14 January** – The locomotive the *Flying Scotsman* makes its last scheduled run
- **18 January** – Labour Leader Hugh Gaitskell dies
- **29 January** – French President Charles de Gaulle vetoes the UK's entry into the European Economic Community (EEC)

FEBRUARY

- **11 February** – The Beatles record their debut album '*Please Please Me*' in a single session
- **14 February** – Harold Wilson is elected Leader of the Labour Party

MARCH

- **4 March** – In Paris, six people are sentenced to death for conspiring to assassinate President Charles de Gaulle. De Gaulle pardons five of them, but the leader of the plot is executed by firing squad a few days later
- **21 March** – The Alcatraz Island Federal Penitentiary in San Francisco Bay closes. The last twenty-seven prisoners

are transferred elsewhere on the orders of Attorney General Robert F. Kennedy
- **27 March** – Dr Beeching issues a report calling for huge cuts to the UK's rail network

APRIL

- **6 April** – Polaris Sales Agreement signed with the USA
- **9 April** – Sir Winston Churchill becomes honorary citizen of the USA
- **12 April** – Martin Luther King, Ralph Abernathy, Fred Shuttlesworth and others are arrested in a Birmingham, Alabama protest for 'parading without a permit'
- **15 April** – 70,000 marchers arrive in London from Aldermarston to demonstrate against nuclear weapons
- **16 April** – Martin Luther King issues his *Letter from Birmingham Jail*

MAY

- **2 May** – Thousands of African-Americans, many of them children, are arrested while protesting against segregation in Birmingham, Alabama. Public Safety Commissioner Eugene 'Bull' Connor later unleashes fire hoses and police dogs on the demonstrators
- **8 May** – *Dr No*, the first James Bond film, is released in the USA
- **9 May** – The Army of the Republic of Vietnam opens fire on Buddhists who defy a ban on the flying of the Buddhist flag
- **11 May** – Everton win the Football League Championship
- **15 May** – Tottenham Hotspur win the European Cup Winners' Cup by beating Athletico Madrid 5-1 in the final
- **25 May** – Manchester United win the FA Cup by beating Leicester City 3-1 at Wembley

JUNE

- **5 June** – War Minister John Profumo resigns from the government and Parliament
- **11 June** – In Saigon, a Buddhist monk commits self-immolation in protest against the oppression of Buddhists by the government of Ngo Dinh Diem
- **11 June** – Governor George C. Wallace stands in the door of the University of Alabama to protest against integration, before stepping aside and allowing African-Americans James Hood and Vivian Malone to enroll
- **11 June** – President John F. Kennedy delivers an historic Civil Rights address, in which he promises a Civil Rights Bill
- **16 June** – Soviet cosmonaut Valentina Tereshkova is the first woman in space on board *Vostok 6*
- **21 June** – Pope Paul VI succeeds Pope John XXIII as the 262nd pope
- **26 June** – John F. Kennedy gives his 'Ich bin ein Berliner' speech in West Berlin

JULY

- **7 July** – Kim Philby is named as the 'Third Man' in the Burgess and Maclean spy ring. His defection to the Soviet Union is confirmed
- **12 July** – Pauline Reade, 16, is abducted and murdered by Myra Hindley and Ian Brady in Manchester
- **30 July** – The Soviet government announce that Kim Philby has been granted political asylum

AUGUST

- **5 August** – The USA, UK and Soviet Union sign a Nuclear Test Ban Treaty
- **8 August** – The Great Train Robbery takes place at Cheddington, Buckinghamshire

- **18 August** – American Civil Rights Movement: James Meredith becomes the first black person to graduate from the University of Mississippi
- **21 August** – Cable 243: in the wake of the Xa Loi Pagoda raids, the Kennedy Administration orders the US Embassy in Saigon to explore alternative leadership in South Vietnam, opening the way for a coup against Diem
- **28 August** – Martin Luther King delivers his 'I have a dream' speech on the steps of the Lincoln Memorial

SEPTEMBER

- **5 September** – Model Christine Keeler is arrested for perjury. On 6 December she is sentenced to nine months in prison
- **15 September** – American Civil Rights Movement: The 16th Street Baptist Church bombing in Birmingham, Alabama kills four and injures twenty-two
- **17 September** – RAF Fylingdales, the ballistic missile early warning radar station on the North Yorkshire Moors, becomes operational
- **23 September** –The Robbins Report on Higher Education is published; it recommends that university places should be available to all those who are qualified for them by ability and attainment
- **24 September** – The US Senate ratifies the Nuclear Test Ban Treaty
- **25 September** – The Denning Report on the Profumo Affair is published by Her Majesty's Stationery Office (HMSO)

OCTOBER

- **10 October** – Prime Minister Harold Macmillan announces that he will resign as soon as a successor has been chosen
- **10 October** – The second James Bond film, *From Russia with Love*, opens in London

- **19 October** – Sir Alec Douglas Home succeeds Harold Macmillan as prime minister

NOVEMBER

- **2 November** – South Vietnamese coup: South Vietnamese President Ngo Dinh Diem is assassinated following a military coup
- **6 November** – Vietnam War: coup leader General Duong Van Minh takes over as leader of South Vietnam
- **22 November** – The Beatles' second album, *With The Beatles*, is released
- **22 November** – President John F. Kennedy is assassinated in Dallas, Texas. Governor John B. Connally is seriously wounded, and Vice President Lyndon B. Johnson becomes the thirty-sixth president
- **23 November** – John Kilbride, 12, is abducted and murdered by Myra Hindley and Ian Brady in Manchester
- **23 November** – The first episode of the BBC television series *Doctor Who* is broadcast
- **24 November** – President Kennedy's alleged assassin, Lee Harvey Oswald, is shot dead by Jack Ruby in Dallas, Texas on live national television
- **24 November** – President Lyndon B. Johnson confirms that the USA intends to continue supporting South Vietnam militarily and economically
- **25 November** – John F. Kennedy is buried at Arlington National Cemetery
- **29 November** – President Lyndon B. Johnson establishes the Warren Commission to investigate the assassination of President Kennedy

DECEMBER

- **3 December** – The Warren Commission begins its investigation
- **21 December** – Cyprus Emergency: inter-communal fighting erupts between Greek Cypriots and Turkish Cypriots

1

JANUARY – Ice Box Britain

Newspaper headlines have a habit of describing bad weather as the worst in the century, or since records began in 1659. But the winter of 1962/63 really was unforgettably cold. Within living memory, only the winter of 1947 has rivalled it for sheer misery. In 1963, just eighteen years after the war, most people still did not have central heating or cars, and shortages of fuel and power made life grim. The number of people dying of the usual winter illnesses rose dramatically in the first three months of the year.

It started unremarkably enough, with light snow on 20 November. The first few days of December saw temperatures fall below freezing, despite the sunshine, which was followed by thick, often freezing, fog. (Implementation of the 1956 Clean Air Act was gradual; in some towns coal still caused major pollution and reduced air quality.)

On the afternoon of Boxing Day, snow drifted down in huge flakes and began to settle. By early evening, frozen points at Crewe were delaying trains from the north, creating a tailback of trains at signals further up the line; the Glasgow–London train was among them. When

17

signals forced it to wait in the dark at a point some way past Winslow, the driver found that the phone didn't work at the Coppenhall signal-box ahead and chose to ignore a red light. He drove his train slowly past it to the next signal-box. What he could not see, in darkness through swirling snow, was a stationary train ahead; the 16.45 from Liverpool–Birmingham. He collided with the back of it at about 20mph; its rear coaches were telescoped, killing eighteen and injuring thirty-four.

More thick snow fell every day until 29 December, when blizzards began. Local councils up and down the country were kept busy salting the roads; snowdrifts were 3ft deep and in most places travel by car was impossible. People postponed journeys by road, but the weather didn't improve; trains were delayed all over the country. Pipes were frozen and local authorities had to open stand-pipes in the roads. Householders – usually the women – trudged through the snow to these and filled buckets several times a day. Without a stand-pipe they could not wash, flush lavatories or cook, and disposable nappies for babies were too expensive for most mothers then, even if they had access to them.

Freezing temperatures did not abate. Snow blanketed the whole of Britain until the end of January, and lay thick until March in some areas. Snow was reported to be 6in deep in Manchester city centre, 9in deep in Leeds and about 18in in Birmingham. By the end of January, the sea had frozen for 1 mile out from shore at Herne Bay in Kent. From Windsor upstream, the Thames was frozen from bank to bank. To make matters worse, members of the militant Electrical Trades Union (ETU) began to 'work to rule' in power stations. Power cuts closed cinemas and theatres, and prevented floodlit football fixtures, not that many matches could have been played; most were called off because of frozen pitches. Street lighting flickered and traffic lights stopped working. The roads were dangerous already, with people falling over and cars skidding or getting stuck. A country accustomed to using public transport found it too cold to wait for a bus. Trains were constantly delayed by frozen points.

To keep roads open at all, councils had frozen snow shovelled onto lorries and piled up on open land. Salting the roads became ineffective as it required a certain amount of traffic to mix it in and melt the ice and snow; this traffic failed to arrive, especially at night and at weekends when temperatures were very low.

Icy weather soon began to affect the economy; food prices rose. The average wage was £16 per week, a working person's often closer to £12. Tomatoes and Cox's apples went up to sixpence a pound; eggs were a shocking four and six (about 24p) a dozen; and potatoes sevenpence per pound.

Between 21 and 25 January, freezing fog returned, which made driving particularly dangerous. Diesel fuel froze, studding the highways with broken down vehicles. The cold spell was in its fifth week when the ETU's work to rule ended, but it took some time for normal service to resume and power cuts persisted in the meantime.

When a thaw did set in, water mains burst; according to some reports, 200,000 gallons of water a day were pouring to waste in towns and cities as a result of leaks and broken mains. And with the end of January, the cold weather returned. Throughout the first week of February there was heavy snow and storms, with gale-force winds reaching Force 8 on the Beaufort scale. A thirty-six-hour blizzard caused heavy drifts that were 20ft deep in some areas. Midwives, district nurses, emergency doctors and NHS staff – like everyone else – struggled to work through it all.

Where cars could still drive, they were being affected by road salt, rust and corrosion. The press reported that old paraffin heaters were being brought out and used, causing fires. People knocked them over or tried to refill them without turning them off first, causing a horrible whoosh of flame and setting themselves and their home alight; fire brigades were kept busy.

The 1 March, said the papers excitedly, was 'the warmest day since November', but temperatures descended below freezing again at night. However, the spring thaw really had begun now, and on 5 March no frost was recorded in the morning and the last traces of the Boxing Day snow had vanished. On 8 March it rained; on 13 March, crocuses bloomed; and on 6 April, there were daffodils. The daffodils appeared six weeks later than usual.

Sports fixtures resumed. Football was way behind schedule, with some FA Cup matches having been postponed as many as ten times, and some league sides had every fixture cancelled between 8 December and 16 February. When spring came, they played three times a week to catch up. Rugby (Union and League) was much the same. As for horse racing, which had seen not a single race between 23 December and 7 March, it was a very bad year for bookies.

Britain breathed a sigh of relief, for it had been a dreadful winter.

Death of Hugh Gaitskell

The Leader of the Labour Party, Hugh Gaitskell, died on the evening of 18 January 1963 at the age of 56 after a short illness. As Leader of the Opposition for the past seven years, he was, by common consent, almost on the threshold of 10 Downing Street. By the end of 1962, not only his own party, but a good many Conservatives, expected him to be prime minister before the next autumn.

He had had an interesting background: Winchester and Oxford, a certain radicalisation as a result of the General Strike, and a career as an academic economist, which included the momentous years of 1933 and '34 in Vienna. He spent the war years working with Hugh Dalton at the Ministry of Economic Warfare, which ran the Special Operations Executive (SOE) whose personnel assisted in sabotaging the Axis powers overseas.

Gaitskell was elected Labour MP for Leeds South at the 1945 General Election, which Labour won by a landslide. Promotion came quickly and within two years he was appointed to the Cabinet as Minister of Fuel and Power. When Sir Stafford Cripps fell ill and had to resign as Chancellor of the Exchequer, Gaitskell was chosen to take his place. This was seen at the time as the result of Hugh Dalton's influence, and Gaitskell turned out to be a controversial chancellor; the National Health Service (NHS), the jewel in Labour's crown since its inception in 1948, suddenly imposed charges for prescription spectacles and false teeth. (One reason for the charges was that Britain, which was still broke, with food rationing and a huge demand for housing, was required to contribute to the funding of the Korean War.) Aneurin Bevan, Harold Wilson and John Freeman resigned over the prescription charges, which they felt violated the fundamental principle of the NHS, and from then on there was recurrent conflict between Left and Right in the party.

Labour was defeated in 1951, and again in 1955, and after that second defeat Clement Attlee resigned as Party Leader; Gaitskell beat Aneurin Bevan and Herbert Morrison to the post.

Gaitskell was forceful in opposition; in particular during the Suez Crisis in 1956. President Nasser of Egypt had suddenly nationalised the Suez Canal, a route of enormous importance to world trade. Israel invaded, and Britain and France issued an ultimatum to both countries; when Nasser failed to respond, they bombed Cairo. This was a terrible move, carried out without the support of the United Nations (UN). The Russians, who supported Nasser, were furious; the Americans were appalled; and the British and French were forced to retire with ignominy. It turned out that Britain and France had orchestrated the entire episode with the Israelis in the first place. Gaitskell was scathing in Parliament, and he had public support.

Nevertheless, Labour failed yet again to win in 1959. Notwithstanding the Festival of Britain, people still associated the Labour Party with the grey years of post-war impoverishment and the Conservatives exploited that with their slogan: 'Life's better with the Conservatives! Don't let Labour ruin it.'

Gaitskell did not prevaricate: he knew what he wanted. On every issue, you knew where you were with him and it was unlikely to be on the Left. The major exception to this rule was his stance on the Common Market. Macmillan was trying to get Britain in, but Gaitskell, like the Left of the Labour Party, opposed him because he said the country would lose its independence: it would be 'the end of a thousand years of British history'.

Bevan, Wilson and others on the Left proclaimed rigid commitment to nationalisation, as under Clause 4 of the Party's constitution:

> ... to secure for the workers by hand or by brain the full fruits of their industry and the most equitable distribution thereof that may be possible upon the basis of the common ownership of the means of production, distribution and exchange, and the best obtainable system of popular administration and control of each industry or service.

Gaitskell was flexible on nationalisation, and he also refused to commit Labour to the Campaign for Nuclear Disarmament's aim of unilateral disarmament.

He was due to visit the Soviet Union in the New Year of 1963. He had had the flu in December, but was pronounced fit to travel; after all he had recovered and was younger than Attlee, Eden or Macmillan had been when they took office.

However, immediately after Christmas, he fell ill again, and the trip to meet Nikita Khrushchev had to be cancelled. On 4 January he was admitted to the Middlesex Hospital with what turned out, two days later, to be serious kidney trouble. On 17 January, an unsuccessful kidney transplant was performed; there were repeated attempts at dialysis, but his heart and lungs seemed too weak to stand the strain. At 9.10 p.m. on 18 January, his organs suffered a total failure and he died; his wife Dora was by his side.

Messages flooded in from the queen, Kennedy, Khrushchev, Lord Attlee and national leaders all over the world, many of whom had expected that, after the 1964 British election, Gaitskell would be prime minister. Then the conspiracy theory began.

Dr Somerville, from the Middlesex Hospital, thought there was something fishy going on. Three days later he contacted MI5; its Director General, Roger Hollis, was immediately interested. Anatoli Golytsin, a recent defector from Russia, had revealed that the KGB was planning a political assassination in Europe in order to replace the victim with a man of their choice. Hollis suggested that Arthur Martin, Head of the Russian Counter-espionage section, should find out what Dr Somerville had to say.

Dr Somerville told him that Gaitskell had died of *lupus disseminata*. This, he apparently said, was an extremely rare disease, almost unknown in temperate climates, and in the past year Gaitskell had not been anywhere where he could have caught it.

Martin consulted the Government's Chemical and Microbiological Laboratory at Porton Down in Sussex, where Dr Bill Ladell, who was very knowledgeable about chemical and biological warfare, said that nobody knew how *lupus disseminata* was transmitted. It might be a fungus, but that didn't help in knowing how it was contracted. Martin then asked the CIA to find out from Russian scientific papers whether the Soviet agencies might have considered using lupus surreptitiously to bring about death. They sent MI5 an English translation of a 1958 Russian scientific journal which described the use of a chemical that the Russians had discovered that could induce lupus in experimental rats; however, the quantities required to produce lupus were considerable and had to be given repeatedly. Dr Ladell, having read a copy of the CIA's response, suggested that if the Russians had continued their lupus research in the five years since they produced the paper, they may well have found a more effective form of the chemical, requiring much smaller doses.

The story seems unlikely. Gaitskell was surely less of a threat to socialism than the Tories; why choose to assassinate him unless they were sure they had their own man ready to take his place? But Harold Wilson, his successor, followed the usual path of radicals in office, demonstrating by compromise that politics is the art of the possible.

However he died, Gaitskell's reputation also remains subject to debate. Would 1960s Britain have fared any better under the leadership of such a man, fabled for his principles, as opposed to Wilson? Harold Wilson, by the early 1970s, was viewed by many as an unprincipled chameleon. A conviction politician some twenty years before conviction politics became the vogue, Gaitskell could well be seen as a politician ahead of his time. Had he lived, he might have won a larger majority in 1964 than Harold Wilson. Even with a smaller win, it seems likely that he would have pushed ahead with a tougher, more radical agenda than the more cautious Wilson. On economic policy, for example, he would doubtless have gone ahead and devalued the pound within months of the election (unlike Wilson, who did not grasp the nettle until late 1967). Gaitskell would also have pushed through legislation to curb unofficial 'wild-cat' strikes, if necessary risking a head-on conflict with the Trade Union Movement. Being a virulent anti-marketeer, he could well have vetoed any further moves by Britain to seek membership. In his day, though, the gift of Common Market membership was still very much in the hands of the French, who four days before his death made their views on the matter profoundly clear.

'Non'

When France, West Germany, Italy, Belgium, Luxembourg and Holland formed the Common Market in 1958, Britain feared membership would have too severe an impact on its Commonwealth markets, which still counted for a large part of the nation's trade.

Instead, the Macmillan government opted to create a rival, looser free trade area with the Scandinavian countries, plus Portugal and Switzerland, which was collectively known as the European Free Trade Area or EFTA. Within five years, however, the economic remedies employed by Macmillan and his chancellor, Selwyn Lloyd, failed to have any real impact on Britain's growing inability to match the economic growth and rise in living standards being achieved by the six Common Market countries. Fearing he may have missed the European boat, Macmillan began a round of diplomacy, which culminated in an announcement in 1961 that Britain desired to seek membership to the Common Market.

Having previously been invited to join, and having (so far as the rest of Europe was concerned) arrogantly rejected the offer, Macmillan was now having to apply from a position of weakness. In particular, he encountered scepticism from France and, to a lesser extent, from West Germany. Both saw Britain as half-hearted in its commitment to the ideals of European unity and feared Britain's continuing close ties with the United States.

This European wariness became apparent in December 1962, when Macmillan held talks with French president Charles de Gaulle. Macmillan discovered that, far from mellowing, de Gaulle had become more intransigent. Britain, he thundered, had not yet thrown off its old bonds with the United States, and Macmillan had failed to convince him that he was prepared to be a good European rather than an apologist for the Americans. Why, then, Macmillan muttered as he listened to this, had the French allowed the talks to drag on for so many weary months if they were opposed to the British application all along?

On 14 January 1963, at an Elysée Palace press conference, de Gaulle humiliated Macmillan by announcing his reservations to a worldwide audience: 'England is insular,' he boomed to the assembled media, 'bound up by her trade, her markets, her food supplied by the most varied and often the most distant countries ... In short, the nature and structure and economic context of England differ profoundly from those of the other states of the Continent.' Should Britain be allowed to join the Common Market, he continued, 'in the end there would appear a colossal Atlantic community under American dependence and leadership which would soon swallow up the European Community.' He had, he concluded, decided to veto Britain's application.

Macmillan sought to redress matters by making a live television broadcast on BBC and ITV the following day. With the very picture of patrician composure, he admitted that 'a great opportunity has been missed', but was quick to blame the 'misguided' de Gaulle for the failure. The perceived half-heartedness of Macmillan's application had undoubtedly made it easier for de Gaulle to oppose it. Macmillan's chance of success might have been better had he applied for membership immediately after the 1959 election, when his popularity and prestige were at their height, and when the French president's personal position at home was still weak and uncertain. Having missed that opportunity, Macmillan had compounded his European difficulties by pressing ahead with nuclear weapons co-operation talks with President Kennedy in December 1962. These could easily have been postponed until after his talks at the beginning of January with de Gaulle.

That aside, the responsibility for the foundering of the application ultimately lay with de Gaulle, not with Macmillan. The news of the veto was, if anything, greeted with relief by a large section of the British public, along with the majority of the popular press. 'Glory, glory, Hallelujah!' proclaimed the *Daily Express*. 'It's all over; Britain's Europe bid is dead. This is not a day of misery at all. It is a day of rejoicing, a day when Britain has failed to cut its own throat.'

Macmillan's chief negotiator, Edward Heath, continued to believe that Common Market membership would be the economic panacea to Britain's troubles. He would eventually secure entry for Britain in 1972, albeit on less favourable terms than those sought in 1961–62. Ironically, the United States, whose silent shadow had hung over Britain's application from the start, was about to change course on the other side of the world. President Kennedy, who had encouraged Macmillan to seek membership partly because he saw the Common Market as a positive move away from European colonialism, was about to embark on a crippling colonial war many thousands of miles away in a former French colony in South East Asia.

Vietnam: the Battle of Ap Bac

'We've got them in a trap,' growled US General Paul D. Harkins, 'and we're going to spring it in half an hour.' He was talking about a unit of Communist Viet Cong fighters in the South Vietnamese hamlet of Ap Bac. *New York Times* correspondent David Halberstam made a note; he had asked Harkins to comment on rumours of a skirmish, and had inadvertently stumbled on a story that would typify the forthcoming decade of news coverage in Vietnam.

The situation in Vietnam had been deteriorating for years, after the country had been split into North and South in 1954. Under the Geneva Accords of that year, the general idea was that Communist sympathisers would move north, and the rest would go south, and in the end there would be one Vietnam with a democratically elected government, living more or less in harmony. Ho Chi Minh, now an old man and no longer Party Leader, but still a figure of influence, was still banking on an election that would unite the two sides. The South Vietnamese Government was in no hurry to hold one since they feared the Communists would win.

Meanwhile, in the paddy fields and forests of the south, militant Communists who should have moved north still remained. They had formed the Viet Cong to fight a guerrilla war against the hated South Vietnamese regime, headed by President Ngo Dinh Diem. Towards the end of 1962, Diem had launched an anti-Communist offensive aimed at driving out a small band of Viet Cong fighters embedded in the jungles of South Vietnam. The Viet Cong were on their own, as the North Vietnamese rejected taking any military action which might incite the United States to intervene in support of Diem.

President Diem's new campaign was showing early signs of success, and the Viet Cong, however disadvantaged, had to do something. At first they simply retreated to increasingly remote hamlets in the hills and river estuaries of South Vietnam. Poorly trained, ill-motivated and ill-equipped South Vietnamese forces took several days to get anywhere near them, and simply allowed themselves to be led deep into territory in which they could easily be encircled. Strategically, chasing the Viet Cong was pointless.

American 'advisors' had begun arriving in South Vietnam early on in the Kennedy Administration. In fact, they were Special Forces who took an active involvement in the conflict from its inception, aided and abetted by effective CIA intelligence. But at last the Pentagon began to supply helicopters, which changed the nature of the conflict considerably by allowing South Vietnamese forces to fly to almost any part of the country where they spotted a Viet Cong presence. The helicopters, as well as new armoured personnel carriers (APCs), took a heavy toll on Viet Cong units from late 1962 onwards. The lightly armed Viet Cong had no weapons capable of stopping the APCs and were forced to flee, suffering heavy casualties.

Yet, they did get away, as South Vietnamese officers were often reluctant to risk their lives chasing Viet Cong. This frustrated the CIA, who saw timidity as a lack of commitment.

In the first few days of 1963, the CIA deployed even more advanced technology. American aircraft with eavesdropping equipment searched for Viet Cong radio transmitters and met with almost immediate success. They intercepted Viet Cong radio signals from the hamlet of Ap Tan Thoi; clearly this was a guerrilla command centre. CIA analysts reported that the Viet Cong were planning to deploy about 120 men to defend their radio transmitter, which was a captured American model.

US intelligence had tracked down Viet Cong wth transmitters before, but they had usually melted into the landscape before South Vietnamese soldiers could get to them. The CIA knew where the Viet Cong were, but they didn't know that they'd changed their policy. They weren't going to play 'come and get me' any more; the next time the South Vietnamese came looking for them, they intended to stand their ground and fight.

On 2 January, the South Vietnamese had about 320 troops, including Civil Guard, in Ap Bac and Ap Tan Thoi. At 4.00 a.m., Viet Cong scouts reported hearing truck engines close to Ap Bac and, as a result, the Viet Cong dug in while the villagers fled to hide in nearby swamps.

The CIA estimated that thirty Shawnee helicopters were needed to airlift the entire South Vietnamese force into the area where the Viet Cong were thought to be. As just ten were apparently available, only one company at a time could be flown into the battlefield. At around 7.00 a.m., the first helicopters dropped off some local Civil Guards. The regular South Vietnamese army units arrived late, so after a while the Civil Guards set off for Ap Tan Thoi. As they approached Ap Bac, Viet Cong radio operators tracked their movements. These they relayed to Viet Cong troops who opened fire from their foxholes, killing the Civil Guard company commander and inflicting heavy casualties. Survivors cowered well below the bullets in a nearby dike. From the unpleasant depths of the ditch, they couldn't let US co-ordinators know whether the South Vietnamese army following them were firing into the right place. As a consquence, artillery rounds continued to fall well behind Viet Cong positions.

CIA-trained pilots in L-19 aircraft now flew over the area where they believed the Viet Cong were entrenched; the Viet Cong did nothing, knowing that the pilots were trying to draw fire in order to identify their positions. When they found no sign of the Viet Cong, helicopter pilots descended in order to drop South Vietnamese troops in what they thought was a quiet area. When they were hovering above ground and troops were jumping out, Viet Cong fire disabled the craft, which crashed to earth. The Viet Cong then brought down two more approaching helicopters.

A fourth aircraft returned to Ap Bac in an attempt to rescue the downed crews, but was so heavily damaged by anti-aircraft guns that it had to make a forced landing in a nearby paddy field. The Viet Cong had either destroyed or downed four helicopters within less than an hour, increasing the morale of the guerrilla fighters.

At 1.30 p.m., South Vietnamese M-113 APCs closed in on the downed helicopters on the western side of Ap Bac, but approached the landing zone in single file instead of in formation. As a result, the Viet Cong were able to concentrate their fire on one target at a time. The M-113 gun crews were also easy targets for Viet Cong snipers. By the end of the day, fourteen South Vietnamese M-113 crewmen had been killed and eighteen injured. In a last ditch effort to overrun the Viet Cong's stronghold, an M-113 equipped with a flamethrower was sent forward to within 330ft of the Viet Cong position. Although the flamethrower had a range of up to 660ft, when it was actually fired it malfunctioned; the crew had mixed too much jelling agent with the gasoline.

With the failure of their final flawed attack and with morale breaking down, South Vietnamese troops began a disorderly withdrawal. As they waded through the paddy fields the Viet Cong were able to pick them off one by one, and at the same time intercept South Vietnamese paratroopers as their parachutes became entangled in trees. Within a matter of hours the airborne battalion had lost nineteen men, with another thirty-three wounded, along with an undeclared number of Americans who had parachuted in with the South Vietnamese.

Shortly afterwards, and more than eighteen hours too late, South Vietnamese artillery hit Ap Bac, killing five more of their own soldiers and wounding a further fourteen.

A small posse of journalists, including David Halberstam, had been kept well behind the lines all day. But, remembering General Harkins' comment that 'we've got them in a trap', perhaps, they thought, they would see 120 contrite Viet Cong?

On 3 January they were taken to Ap Bac by American military advisors; it was deserted. Reporter Neil Sheehan asked US Brigadier General Robert York what had happened: 'What the hell's it look like happened, boy. They got away, that's what happened.'

When questioned about where the responsibility lay, Lieutenant Colonel John Paul Vann replied, 'It was a miserable damn performance, just like it always is. These people won't listen. They make the same mistake over and over again in the same way.' It was an admission. Yesterday had ended in defeat, not victory, and the Americans despaired of knocking the South Vietnamese army into any kind of shape.

The contrast between the gung-ho optimism of politicians and desk-bound military leaders, and the more candid, down-to-earth views of those in the field was clear to see. Vietnam would ultimately become the first round-the-clock television war in history. Television would continue to expose this gulf between perception and reality, and lead to loss of public support for the Vietnam War in the United States.

The Viet Cong suffered eighteen soldiers killed and thirty-nine wounded, but the Battle of Ap Bac marked the first time they stood and fought, and won, crushing a bigger and better-equipped enemy despite huge odds against them. From then on, they were convinced that the South Vietnamese army, supported by a combination of artillery and armoured units, as well as American airpower, could not beat them; they understood the territory, and they were fighting for a cause.

Ap Bac demonstrated that Diem's lacklustre army was not competent enough to destroy a resurgent Viet Cong, particularly in the Mekong River Delta and Vietnam's many miles of remote forest. For the Americans, it would lead to massive troop commitments in Vietnam and the paralysis of the Johnson Administration from its first to last day.

2

FEBRUARY – Please Please Me

Harold Wilson

The Labour Party leadership election of 1963, held in the aftermath of Hugh Gaitskell's death, resulted in a choice that not only determined the direction of the Labour Party during the late 1960s and early '70s, but that of the country as a whole.

In 1963, the Labour leader was elected by Labour MPs only, in a system called the 'exhaustive ballot'. To win outright, a candidate required more than half the votes in the first ballot. If that didn't happen, then the last placed candidate was eliminated and a new ballot was contested by the remaining candidates. And so it went on until one man finally obtained a majority. Three candidates were declared:

GEORGE BROWN, the shadow home secretary and deputy leader since 1960, was MP for Belper, Derbyshire. He had been a junior minister in the Attlee government. George Brown was popular with the party's grass roots and, as a former official of the Transport and General Workers Union, was particularly well liked within the Trade Union Movement. His campaign stood for the continuation of Gaitskell's right-wing economic and defence policies. Unfortunately, as his Parliamentary colleagues knew only too well, he was often drunk and could be highly volatile.

JAMES CALLAGHAN represented Cardiff South East and was shadow chancellor. He too had been a junior minister under Attlee. Callaghan was also on the party's right wing, but was encouraged to stand by fellow right-wingers who had profound reservations about Brown's capacity to be leader. The Brown camp understandably thought Callaghan's intervention would simply split the right-wing vote.

HAROLD WILSON, the third candidate, was probably the cleverest. He conveyed an impression of pipe-smoking intellectual tranquillity; he had been a don before the war, lived in Hampstead, and his wife was a poet. During the war he had worked in Whitehall, largely as a statistician and economist. He had been MP for two successive Lancashire constituencies since the war: Ormskirk from 1945–1950, and Huyton, Liverpool since 1950. He was shadow foreign secretary and had previously served as Labour's shadow chancellor. He was the only one with Cabinet experience, having been President of the Board of Trade in Attlee's government, and the youngest Cabinet minister in a generation. In 1951, he had proved that he could stick to his principles in a crisis by resigning over Gaitskell's decision to impose NHS charges. Those principles had mellowed a little; he had been a leftist Bevanite then, but was now seen as closer to the centre-left.

For many undecided Labour MPs, the critical moment of the leadership campaign came when Wilson was speaking in a House of Commons debate on the afternoon of 31 January. Gaitskell's memorial service had been held that very morning and Prime Minister Harold Macmillan saw an opportunity to put Wilson on the spot in front of his own MPs. As Brown and Callaghan, who had not performed particularly well in the debate, sat alongside Wilson, Macmillan rose to his feet and pressed him to state clearly whether or not he agreed with a statement Gaitskell had made the previous year on economic policy. If Wilson fudged the answer, Macmillan would have scored a point; if he agreed with Gaitskell's statement, he risked alienating his left-wing supporters; if he disagreed with Gaitskell, he risked alienating the centre-right MPs whose votes he would need if he was to have any chance at all of winning a clear majority of votes.

As Wilson himself later recalled in his memoirs:

I was completely relaxed. I had my feet up on the table, but then stood up and said, 'The Rt Hon Gentleman has correctly quoted what Hugh Gaitskell had said.' I went on to point out to the Prime Minister that Hugh had said that there were two possible approaches to this particular problem and that the Prime Minister had failed to mention the other, which I told him he would find on a particular page of the published version of Hugh Gaitskell's speeches. This for once had Macmillan flurried. He did not have the reference and had no possibility of checking it. I always think this exchange is what really won me the leadership, because what the Labour Party wanted was someone who could put Harold Macmillan down.

The result of the first ballot was declared on 7 February; none of the three got 50 per cent of the votes. Wilson got more than Brown, and Callaghan was eliminated. In the second ballot on 14 February, Wilson got 144 votes to Brown's 103.

Had the bulk of Callaghan's right-wing vote transferred over to Brown then he would have won. However, it was clear from the vote that a good number of Labour MPs, reluctantly in some cases, decided to back Wilson instead, such was their concern at aspects of Brown's character.

He proved to be an inspiring leader, shifting the party's image away from the grey 1950s when he said during the 1963 conference that Britain's future would be forged in 'the white heat of technological revolution'.

Brown never forgave Wilson for, as he saw it, depriving him of the party leadership and, ultimately, the post of prime minister. Wilson positioned himself as a patriotic technocrat from the start. In one of his first interviews as Leader of the Opposition, he told the BBC that he saw Britain's role in the future as being centred on 'economic strength, social justice and a restoration of Britain's moral leadership'. It was on these three issues, Wilson said, 'that the Labour Party will be fighting the next General Election.' In closing the interview, which was hurriedly conducted as he was about to board a train at Euston for his constituency, he was asked if he was at all worried that his first journey as leader was starting from platform 13. He replied, 'No, I'm not superstitious.'

Later on, he did sometimes seem fearful of who-knew-what, but maybe he had a point. Whispers about the alleged Soviet plot to replace 'a European leader' were circulating after Gaitskell's sudden death, and resurfaced years later when maverick MI5 officer Peter Wright published his autobiography *Spycatcher* in 1987. In it he set out the suspicions of a group of right-wing MI5 officers; they always thought, he wrote, that Wilson had Soviet links.

In 2009, when MI5 published its centennial official history, the world discovered that MI5 had indeed kept a file on Wilson, from his entering Parliament in 1945 and throughout his two terms of office as prime minister (1964–70 and 1974–76).

The file was initially opened because of 'concern' about his friends. Over the years he either socialised with, or liked: Joseph Kagan, a refugee from Lithuania via Romania after the end of the war, who had since built his Gannex mackintosh company into a successful business; Eric Miller, a property magnate who was later accused of corruption; and two influential economists, Nicholas Kaldor and Thomas Balogh, who had been born in Hungary. What three of these people had in common was that they were Jewish, and it is more than possible that MI5's suspicions were initially provoked by anti-semitism, although the excuse was that nobody knew enough about Kagan's links behind the Iron Curtain. In the 1950s, Wilson made a significant number of trips to countries of the Eastern Bloc. Looking back, others saw this as a mere indication of his determination to build a reputation as a Russian expert and strengthen his eventual claim to the post of foreign secretary.

Wilson's dossier was so sensitive that it was filed under the name 'Norman John Worthington.' In March 1974, on Wilson's return to office, MI5's Director-General Sir Michael Hanley took additional steps to conceal the Worthington file by instructing that the card referring to it should be removed from the Registry Central Index. Thus, it was made to disappear; if you knew where to look, you still wouldn't find it.

After the collapse of the USSR in 1991, it turned out that the KGB had held a file on Wilson, too. In the early 1950s, they had spotted him as a potential recruit, but after a number of informal overtures they finally dismissed him as a 'right-wing careerist'.

A coup in Iraq

Ba'athism, as a political ideology, had its origins in Arab determination to rid the Middle East of foreign imperialists. Historically, these had usually been Ottoman Turks or British. The Ba'athist Party was formed in Syria after the Second World War. It stood for pan-Arabism, Arab nationalism, socialism and anti-imperialism, and had some success in the 1950s in creating a United Arab Republic of Syria and Egypt, which lasted three years from 1958 to 1961.

On the whole, though, the pacifying of the Arab world proved a rather difficult challenge. The impoverished British colonialists still sought influence; the Americans were looking at the oil; the Russians wanted a strategic and ideological foothold; some of these states had been formed by Europeans drawing arbitrary lines on a map; every individual put his own clan loyalties first; some were in conflict over political ideologies imported from the West; some leaders of Arab states demanded a union of monarchies; others wanted republics, or despotic power; and some were consumed by anger concerning the State of Israel. Islamic extremism had not yet fallen into the mix, but 'melting pot' doesn't even come close. The Middle East was way beyond any hope of lasting peace.

Iraq, the cradle of civilisation and massive exporter of oil, was led by General al Qasim, who had deposed a king and declared Iraq a republic in 1958. His key opponents were in two camps: the Communists, who looked to the USSR for assistance, and the Ba'athists, who wanted to unite with Egypt. Of more immediate concern, by 1963 he was engaged in an ongoing struggle to quell rebellious Kurdish fighters, the Peshmerga, in the north.

His relationships with fellow members of the military leadership had worsened over time, principally over matters of foreign and defence policy. Qasim had part-nationalised IPC, the Iraq Petroleum Company, and was, apparently, hoping to make friendly overtures to the Soviet Union and conclude a strategic defence treaty with the Warsaw Pact. The USA knew a proto-Commie when they saw one, offered financial assistance to the Ba'athists, and made sure that Qasim was overthrown before he could progress any further.

The coup had been planned since 1962, but had been abandoned twice for fear of discovery. The first, on 18 January, was rescheduled for 25 January, the last day before Ramadan, but Qasim found out and arrested some of the principal conspirators. He knew perfectly well that the CIA was complicit in the plot. It is possible that he even knew the Ba'athists, who did not have overwhelming public support and therefore needed all the help they could get, had been communicating with the CIA for years from their Baghdad headquarters.

Action finally began in the early morning of 8 February 1963, fourteenth day of Ramadan, with the assassination of the Communist air force chief and tank units taking over Abu Ghrayb radio station. Qasim retreated to the Ministry of Defence building while his supporters and many Communists fought against Ba'athists in the streets.

At 10.00 a.m. on 9 February, Qasim telephoned the Ba'athist General al-Bakr and offered to surrender in return for safe passage out of the country. His request was refused, and later that afternoon he was captured and given a mock trial over Baghdad radio by the Ba'ath Party's National Council of the Revolutionary Command (NCRC). He was sentenced to death for treason and shot. His bullet riddled body was shown on Iraqi television that evening, Colonel Arif was proclaimed president and General al-Bakr became prime minister.

The most direct evidence of US complicity in what was later called 'The Ramadan Revolution' is a memo from National Security Committee staff member Bob Komer to President John F. Kennedy on the evening of 7 February. The memo indicates prior knowledge of the coup and confirms American financial support for the Ba'ath Party.

The CIA also assured the Ba'ath Party of speedy American recognition of their assumption of power, and military support afterwards. They provided a comprehensive list of names of active Communists, and Ba'ath supporters used this to arrest, torture and kill some 5,000 people in the weeks after the coup.

Four weeks later, on 8 March, a second Ba'ath Party coup occurred in neighbouring Syria. It was led by a group of disgruntled military officers that included Captain Hafiz al-Asad. Hafiz al-Asad became president of Syria in 1971 and ruled until his death in 2000, when his son Basha Hafez al-Asad succeeded him.

While two revolutions in the Middle East were consolidating in the early months of 1963, a revolution of a very different kind was about to break out in Britain.

Brian Epstein and the Mersey Sound

The 'charts' – weekly estimated sales figures of pop hits throughout the UK – played a significant part in youth culture in 1963. Teenagers got pocket money or had Saturday jobs, and the boys, especially, spent it on records they'd heard on Radio Luxembourg. (Girls, who had to buy nylons and eye-shadow as well, spent less, on the whole, on music.) The records teenagers bought were mostly vinyl singles (with an A side and a B side; you had to flip the thing over and put the needle onto it again to play the B side) or EPs (extended play, that is, two songs per side). The record player of choice was the Dansette portable, a must-have in cream bakelite and red leatherette that you could lug along to parties, if required.

On 16 February, the Top Twenty was headed by Frank Ifield singing *The Wayward Wind*. Ifield was a 26-year-old Australian in a bad suit whose songs featured a kind of yodel. The Beatles' *Please Please Me* was on its way up. It shared the list with Acker Bilk, Bobby Vee, the Tornados, the Bachelors, Frankie Vaughan, Jet Harris, Del Shannon, Joe Brown and his Bruvvers, Cliff Richard, the Springfields, Kenny Ball and his Jazzmen, and other English, Australian and American artists. It was a mixture of pop, traditional jazz and ballads, with a few banging instrumentals and an occasional girl group thrown in.

The trajectory of a career in pop music was brief. Ideally, you got your act together, honed it in clubs, works dances or holiday camps, found an agent and a manager, got a recording contract, toured the country and, if you were very lucky indeed, had a run of hit records. But it was all about fashion, so after a while your act would go out of favour. At this point, you would start declaring an interest in becoming 'an all-round entertainer'. This meant a few years of coming second, then third on the bill, a panto and, with luck, by the time you were 35 you'd have enough money left to open a pub.

On 22 February, in an inside page, the *Daily Express* held its nose and deigned to investigate a curious phenomenon they called 'the sound of Scouse'. The reporter identified it as 'rhythm and blues', although *Express* readers probably weren't all that familiar with Muddy Waters and it was hard to see the connection between R&B and what sounded a lot like pop. The 'combos' named were Gerry and the Pacemakers, Billy J. Kramer and the Dakotas, and a few others, but as the article pointed out, so far none were widely known outside the north-west of England.

The only exception was The Beatles, who had reached Number 17 in the charts in October with *Love Me Do* and, strangely, were also known in north-western West Germany.

A year from now, two-thirds of Britain would know that The Beatles had learned their trade in Hamburg, but right now the *Express* man didn't know and didn't ask. He did know, though, that the manager behind most of these groups was a young man from Liverpool called Brian Epstein. He wanted to know why the north-west was so particularly responsive to their distinctive sound and asked a recording engineer from Parlophone called George Martin. George Martin gave the matter serious thought and said it was because Liverpool had 'a concentrated population with English, American, Welsh and Irish influences'. And there the matter rested; although had the *Express* man bothered to look again, he would have found that The Beatles, who had been Number 13 last week, took the Number 1 spot the following day. Could there be more to this than he had noticed?

The year 1963 would be great for Brian Epstein, who had already signed several Liverpool acts. His stable of artists held the Number 1 spot for thirty-two out of fifty-two weeks, and broke the grip that American music had held on the British music industry and music-buying public (a lot of previous hits by British artists had even been cover versions of American songs). For the first time ever, no American artist reached Number 1 that year.

Brian Epstein was 29 and had been born in Liverpool. At 16 he'd begun work at the family's furniture store, I. Epstein & Sons, in Walton. At 18 came conscription to National Service; he was discharged within a year because the army said he was emotionally and mentally unfit to serve, which was code for an incident in which he had 'impersonated an officer'.

In 1954, 20-year-old Brian began to manage Clarendon Furnishing in Hoylake, another Epstein family business, but his family seem to have understood that life in retail was never going to be enough. In 1956 he enrolled at RADA (the Royal Academy for Dramatic Arts) in London to train as an actor. It wasn't for him. A year later he was back in Liverpool, managing a new branch of his father's thriving business, the North End Music Store (NEMS) in Liverpool city centre.

This was a bit more like it. NEMS had musical instruments, television sets and radios for sale on the ground floor, but the young Epstein saw the potential of a gramophone department selling records and record

37

players; rock n'roll was booming in the late '50s, with a lot of American artists like Chuck Berry, Buddy Holly, Bill Haley and the Comets, and, of course, Elvis, all having huge success with teenagers.

Record sales were pretty soon driving profits at the store and he opened another branch, a short distance from the Cavern Club in Matthew Street. He also promoted NEMS by writing a weekly column on records in a local fanzine called *Mersey Beat*, which began in July 1961.

At the end of 1961, Epstein – who didn't normally visit the Cavern, but could spot an opportunity when it came his way – saw The Beatles performing there; saw how the audience went wild for them; liked their quirky outlook and offered to manage them. Six months later, after being rejected by virtually every major record label in Britain, they got signed to EMI's Parlophone label by George Martin; that same George Martin referred to in the article of February 1963 as a 'recording engineer'. He was; but he was a lot more than that.

Brian Epstein backed the Beatles financially for months, which is why he felt he could demand a good deal (25 per cent) as their manager when they eventually signed with him. Yet he wasn't so sure of his own opinion at the start that he didn't back most of the other horses in the race as well. Gerry and the Pacemakers, who had also signed to him, had three consecutive Number 1 hits, the last of which, *You'll Never Walk Alone*, became the Liverpool Football Club anthem in perpetuity. Billy J. Kramer and the Dakotas did well. Billy J. Kramer, Epstein announced, would 'take up where Elvis left off'.

In due course, all these artists flew high but quite quickly sank back into earth's orbit, in the traditional arc of pop achievement; but not The Beatles. Brian Epstein always put them first, probably because two of them were prolific songwriters and he saw that their talent would give them a much longer professional life. Many Epstein artists built their careers on hit songs written by Lennon and McCartney, and between September and December of '63, The Beatles themselves got to Number 1 three times – twice with *She Loves You* (four weeks in September and October, two more at the beginning of December), and again with *I Want to Hold Your Hand*.

Epstein knew how to manage pop bands. He understood the audience from observing them, and he instinctively understood branding. The potential audience was teenage girls from about 13 to 17. As consumers, they were, in 1963, a neglected group. Adults thought of them as children, but they could leave school at 15 and, whether they were at work or at school, most of them had a small but disposable income. The women's magazines, clothes companies and cosmetics companies had not identified this market at all; even Mary Quant was aiming her clothes at an older, elegant girl with money. This was the year when Epstein realised that this cohort of young girls was susceptible to mass hysteria for The Beatles and could be manipulated into producing it, at will, whenever there was a camera or a reporter within range.

But first of all, The Beatles had to be a recognisably different brand. Their music already sounded new and interesting, and in person they had the kind of dry humour that could make them stand out from other young recording artists. They were much brighter and more cynical than most pop singers; they knew exactly what game they were being asked to play and they were up for it. They trusted Epstein. So he quietly got them to drop the uncut hair, art-student jeans and black leather jackets in favour of pudding-bowl haircuts with floppy fringes and collarless, well-cut mod suits. The makeover gave them a puppyish appeal, with an edge. No girl in the target demographic would be ashamed to take a Beatle home to her granny. No granny would recommend switching off the television when The Beatles came on. They were going to be big.

3

MARCH – End of the Line

'Algérie Française'

On 11 March, Jean-Marie Bastien-Thiry became the last person in France to be executed by firing squad. A lieutenant colonel in the French air force, he had been instrumental in the failed plot to assassinate President Charles De Gaulle on 22 August 1962.

He belonged to an organisation called *Vieil Etat-Major* (the Old HQ) which opposed de Gaulle's policy of independence for Algeria. The French, like the British, knew that it was time to divest the mother country of its colonies, but, for historical and constitutional reasons, this seemed to many French people like cutting off a limb. France, unlike Britain, had never had a constitutional divide between its colonies and the mother country. Metropolitan France and its lands overseas together formed the French Republic, and an overseas territory had the political status of a French *département*. French citizens abroad, therefore, voted for representatives to the national assembly in Paris, much as the people of Lanarkshire might vote for an MP to represent them at Westminster. With the move to independence in the 1950s, many expat communities, some of whom had grown up integrated and married in their adopted lands, reluctantly uprooted themselves and returned from Morocco, Tunisia and French Indochina. They had been absorbed back into metropolitan France.

Algeria was particularly difficult because its major cities had so many hundreds of thousands of ethnically French, or mixed, Algerians who were French citizens, popularly known as *pieds noirs* (blackfeet). They had been fighting the decision to cut Algeria adrift since 1954, and there had been protests, bombings and assassinations. Frustrated, they became angrier as time passed, especially when de Gaulle came to power as president in 1958 specifically promising not to allow Algerian independence – and callously betraying their trust.

Early in 1962, the final withdrawal was to be forced upon them. It was the start of a summer of fighting and massacres in Algeria, with Frenchmen on both sides fighting one another.

Some of those who were forced back to metropolitan France belonged to armed and trained right-wing paramilitary groups such as *Organisation de l'Armée Secrète* (OAS) and *Vieil Etat-Major*. A fanatical faction within this minority saw assassination as the only way to force a change at the top and restore the union of France and Algeria. A small group of conspirators decided, therefore, to ambush de Gaulle's car as it sped through the Parisian suburb of Petit-Clamart shortly after 8.00 p.m. on the evening of 22 August.

It would not be the first attempt to kill the president (the final tally came to more than thirty incidents), but Bastien-Thiry had, he thought, planned this one down to the last detail. He would wait along the route and, as the limousine passed, he would wave a newspaper in the air so machine gunners ahead would know the car was about to come into their gunsights. Would they see the newspaper, though? He consulted a calendar to find out when dusk fell on 22 August. It would fall at 8.35 p.m., so he would be seen even if de Gaulle was late.

However, he had missed one crucial detail; he had looked at a 1961 calendar. In 1962, on 22 August, dusk was to fall at 8.10 p.m., so by the time de Gaulle's Citroen DS sped down the Avenue de la Libération at over 60mph, the machine gunners waiting 100yds further on could barely see Bastien-Thiry or his newspaper. Those twenty-five minutes of poor visibility were to change the destiny of France.

As bullets hit the back of his car, de Gaulle apparently exclaimed, 'What, again?'

Miraculously, although the car was raked with machine-gun fire, the president and his wife escaped unhurt. Fourteen bullet holes were found in the car, a further twenty hit a nearby café and another 127 spent shell casings were found on the pavement.

By September, over 700,000 French citizens had left home for good and crossed the Mediterranean to live in France. Once there, the ethnic French rebels did not cease to agitate. On hot nights that summer, Parisians heard the deafening staccato honk of motor horns beating out a defiant Al-gé-rie-Fran-çaise in unison as the *pieds noirs* drove in convoy down the streets.

The other would-be assassins who were arrested and tried alongside Bastien-Thiry were spared the death penalty, as de Gaulle commuted their sentences to life imprisonment. Bastien-Thiry, the leader of the plot, received no such concession. When Bastien-Thiry's lawyer broke the news that de Gaulle had rejected his appeal for clemency, he apparently looked the lawyer in the eye and said, 'You don't understand; no squad of Frenchmen will raise their rifles against me'. At 8.00 a.m. on 11 March, it was announced on French radio bulletins that Bastien-Thiry had been executed by firing squad at Fort d'Ivry in the Parisian suburb of Ivry-sur-Seine.

A decade later, Frederick Forsyth would be inspired to write his bestselling thriller *Day of the Jackal* due to this assassination attempt plotted by Jean-Marie Bastien-Thiry.

Alcatraz: gone, but not forgotten

Alcatraz Federal Penitentiary shut for good on 21 March. As a prison camp, and later a criminal prison of last resort, it had been a symbol of isolation and horror for over a hundred years. From the 1940s onwards, it became notorious all over the world because of Hollywood gangster movies featuring the likes of Humphrey Bogart, James Cagney and George Raft. A mile and a half off the coast of San Francisco, the small island had grown from a lighthouse to a military fortification self-sufficient in many skills and resources; and later to a military prison, prisoner-of-war camp and federal prison.

When California became the thirty-first state of the USA in 1850, in the heat of the California Gold Rush, the US army began to develop Alcatraz Island as a major barracks and armoury, with coastal gun batteries to protect the approaches to San Francisco Bay. Isolated by the dangerous freezing currents of the bay and strongly fortified, Alcatraz was used a decade later to house Confederate prisoners in a guardhouse during the American Civil War. Excavation, construction and improvement were more or less continuous from then on, with the advantage of military prisoners to do the heavy lifting and digging; these were reinforced later by Native Americans captured in skirmishes. In 1867, a brick jailhouse was built. Between 1870 and 1876, plans to construct shell-proof underground tunnels and a safer arsenal were never completed since money ran out, but Alcatraz remained an outstandingly secure prison. Its prison population rose and fell according to military confrontations. At one time during the Spanish Civil War, which began in 1898, 450 men were confined there, and after the San Francisco earthquake its population swelled with convicts from the city jail. They stayed until San Francisco was rebuilt.

Alcatraz was officially recognised as a military establishment for captured or rebellious soldiers. Before the First World War, the Citadel, an old barracks surrounded by a moat and partly built below ground level for better defence, was demolished and subsumed into a huge concrete cell block on top of a basement (the basement gaining notoriety as the site of 'dungeons', which did not exist). During the First World War, conscientious objectors were imprisoned in the new block.

From 1933 onwards, Alcatraz was transferred from the army to the US Department of Justice and the FBI, and, in conjunction with the law of unintended consequences, it began to feature as a Hollywood icon. Gangster movies usually had a bad outcome for the gangsters, and so it was in life. Al Capone, Machine Gun Kelly, Whitey Bulger and many others ended up in Alcatraz, and of course *The Birdman of Alcatraz* was not just a Hollywood movie; Robert Franklin Stroud was a real prisoner who had certainly reared birds in jail. But his bird-keeping days were at Fort Leavenworth and on his release. At Alcatraz, where he spent seventeen years, you didn't have pets. At Alcatraz you were forbidden to speak and were treated, as one later guard said, like a dangerous animal in a zoo. Stroud, judged homicidal, was segregated from the rest of the population for most of the time. The régime was designed by minds with a harsh and embittered outlook for criminals who were a danger to society; most of whom were murderers and some of whom were mad. The guards lived on the island with their families and in many ways lived lives as bad as the prisoners.

Alcatraz was a federal prison for dangerous men that no other jail could hold. The authorities boasted that nobody had ever successfully escaped. Between 1933 and 1963 when it closed, there were fourteen escape attempts, some of them breakouts by small groups of prisoners. Twenty-three were caught and six were shot dead during their escape.

Three escaped and were never found. They got away on 11 June 1962, nine months before Alcatraz shut. They were the Anglin brothers, John and Clarence, and a man called Frank Morris. They figured they could improvise a raft and get away on it, if they could get out of jail. They had noticed some crumbling concrete around an air vent in the cell they shared with another prisoner. Now they had something to live for: a plan. Over many months in 1961, they stole raincoats, from which they would make an inflatable raft, and metal spoons from the canteen. They also managed to purloin a vacuum cleaner motor and from this they fashioned an electric drill. On their block, there was a 'music hour' when they could work under cover of noise. Very slowly and very cautiously, they dug away at the concrete. They had to take a little out, and put it back, so that nobody noticed, until there was a gap big enough to get through. Once this was done, they could cross a utility corridor, get onto the roof through a vent, and descend to the ground.

It took them a year. On the night of 1 June, they escaped. They left a co-conspirator behind, who seems to have lost his nerve, and they were never seen again.

The official investigation by the FBI concluded that the three men had drowned while trying to reach the mainland in the cold and current driven waters of the bay. Friends and family of Morris and the Anglin brothers later claimed they received postcards written in their handwriting. The authorities dismissed these stories as myths perpetrated by publicity-seekers.

In 2011, previously unpublished FBI documents from the 1962 investigation revealed that the raft had been discovered, safely ashore at Angel Island, the day after their escape. There were even footprints leading away from it and a car had been stolen in the area that night. These details were withheld so that the 1962 report could maintain the myth that no one had ever successfully escaped from Alcatraz.

As early as 1952, the then director of the Bureau of Prisons pointed out that a mainland prison would be cheaper to run, and in 1961 many of the buildings were found to be in a dangerous condition due to salt water contamination (the kind of thing that had so conveniently softened the concrete for the 1962 escapees). The metal bars deep within the concrete had corroded. This would cost the Bureau of Prisons $5 million dollars to repair properly. The place was also an environmental disaster, spewing raw sewage into San Francisco Bay and provoking complaints from the city authorities; an efficient sewage disposal system would cost another $5 million.

In Congress, a Californian representative had claimed that it would be cheaper to house the Alcatraz inmates in the Waldorf Astoria with room service than to keep them on 'the Rock'. Attorney General Robert F. Kennedy, who headed the Department for Justice, therefore took the decision to close the prison. Later in the year, the US Penitentiary in Marion, Illinois, a more centrally located prison, opened as a replacement facility for Alcatraz.

Meanwhile, in England, something that had been taken for granted by communities up and down the country for over a century was now also facing the prospect of closure for reasons of economy.

Dr Beeching's Axe

In 1947 Britain's railways had been nationalised. In 1950 they were making money; by 1960, they were losing it hand over fist. In 1961, working losses would be £87 million. That was the year when Richard Beeching, formerly technical director of ICI, was appointed chairman of the new British Railways Board, with a brief to stop the rot; and, on 27 March 1963, he published a report that re-shaped Britain with unintended consequences.

His appointment was recommended by a man seen by many as the real villain of the piece, Ernest Marples. Marples was that unusual animal, a Tory minister who had risen through the ranks: his origins were in the skilled working class, and he had won a scholarship to a grammar school long before the eleven-plus exam existed. He had served in the war and made his fortune out of road-building. In 1959, when (having been postmaster general) he was made minister of transport, there were questions about the fact that a man who was now in charge of the nationalised railways still owned 64,000 of the 80,000 shares in Marples Ridgeway, a road construction company. (He appears to have apologised and sold them to his wife.)

The network was enormous; there was 18,000 miles of it. Branch lines streamed out from cities and linked market towns by way of villages. Almost every train was a 'stopping train', the landowners of the great nineteenth-century country estates having (as a condition of allowing the railway companies to build across their land) insisted on creating a small 'halt' on the line for their weekend guests.

Marples was flamboyant, impatient and cut to the chase; he got things done. In his first year at the Ministry of Transport, traffic wardens and parking restrictions appeared. In 1960 he commissioned 'Traffic in Towns', a report on motor transport which, like Beeching, appeared in 1963. It concluded that, while there were 10.5 million cars on the roads now, there would be 18 million in 1970. Towns would be wrecked by heavy goods vehicles (HGVs), and by too many cars; it was time to build more motorways.

Marples, then, saw rising car ownership as part of a more prosperous future, and thus saw trains as dirty old reminders of the past. Railways needed a dose of businesslike ruthlessness. In 1959 he set up the Stedeford Committee, which was supposed to make recommendations for modernising Britain's transport infrastructure. What its conclusions were, nobody found out; the Stedeford Report was quietly buried for a long time.

But one member of that committee who did impress the minister was Dr Richard Beeching. Beeching, also a man of modest origins, was an extremely bright physicist and life-long ICI man. He was also rather a bean-counter who agreed with Marples that whatever was not economically viable must go. The notion of public service was of vastly lesser importance. Marples saw in Beeching a man whose thinking, formed by the private sector, could bring about a leaner, fitter railway system.

On appointment as chairman of the British Railways Board, Beeching ordered an in-depth review of every aspect of the rail network. In the spring of 1962, he set in motion a study of traffic flows on every railway line in the country. This took place during one week only, the week ending 23 April 1962, two weeks after Easter. It concluded that 30 per cent of the system carried just 1 per cent of passengers and freight, and half of all stations contributed just 2 per cent of income.

The Beeching Report, 'The Reshaping of British Railways', was published at the end of March. Having identified unprofitable lines as the problem, Beeching recommended that such lines should be closed to allow the remaining system to be restored to profitability.

In practice, this meant shutting down one-third of the system (6,000 miles of branch lines, mostly to the rural countryside, and a total of 7,000 stations). Of the remaining 12,000 miles of track, some lines would be kept open for freight only, and many lesser-used stations would be closed on lines that were to be kept open. Buses, Beeching pointed out, would work just as well.

The report was welcomed by the government, but hotly contested by the Labour opposition. Community action groups sprang up the length and breadth of Britain, particularly in rural areas, to protest that they would be cut off without a rail connection; car ownership was by no means universal. The press tended to agree, and championed the rural backlash against the 'Beeching Bombshell' or the 'Beeching Axe'. The government airily promised that abandoned rail services would be replaced by buses, which would be cheaper.

About 3,000 miles of line had already been closed since nationalisation in 1947. After the Beeching Report, closures accelerated markedly. Some lines, listed for closure, were kept open for political reasons: certain railways through the Scottish Highlands were saved by a powerful local lobby, and the Central Wales Line was said to have been kept open because it passed through so many marginal constituencies that no one dared to close it. The Tamar Valley Line in Devon and Cornwall remained because the local roads were so poor, and a few other unprofitable ones were saved for the same reason.

Electorally, Beeching's axe was a disaster, which was added to all the others in 1963. The polls showed that Conservative support was in steady decline and this resulted in backbench pressure when line closures threatened their own constituents. In 1964, during the election campaign, Labour promised to save the branch lines if they got in, but when they did, they made a quick U-turn and closures continued at a faster rate than under the previous administration until 1970.

By then, however, it was clear that closing little-used lines had not hauled the railways out of deficit and never would. By closing almost a third of the rail network, Beeching had managed to save £30 million while losses were running at over £100 million. What he had failed to take into account was that branch lines acted as feeders to main lines, and feeder traffic was lost when the branches closed; there was no point in driving to a main-line station – you might as well drive all the way. Reduced traffic meant reduced income for the increasingly vulnerable main lines.

That was one unintended consequence. The same problem occurred with the movement of goods and freight: without branch lines, the railways' ability to deliver goods almost door-to-door ceased to exist. Beeching had made the unrealistic assumption that lorries would collect goods and transport them to the nearest main-line railway station, where a train would take them to another main station, where another lorry would offload them and continue the journey. But a large part of the M1 was already in use, the M2 had begun, and more motorways were planned; containerisation and improvements in road haulage vehicles would all combine to make long-distance road transport a more viable alternative. Beeching had apparently foreseen none of this.

Another reason why Beeching's plan did not save much money was that many of the closed lines ran at only a small deficit. Some lines, such as one from Sunderland to West Hartlepool, cost only £291 per mile to operate, and shutting this, and other small-scale loss-makers, made little difference. Perhaps, ironically, the busiest commuter routes had always lost most money, but even Beeching realised it would be impractical to close them.

His strategy spectacularly backfired and actually accelerated British Railway's financial losses. More importantly, it was a missed opportunity. In retrospect, a plan put forward by Brigadier Thomas Lloyd DSC MC, in a paper to the Council of the Institution of Civil Engineers in 1955 entitled 'The Potential of the British Railway System as a Reserve Road System', would seem from a twenty-first-century viewpoint to have been a logical and economically sound alternative.

Lloyd's argument was that, although trains could not be made to pay their way on certain parts of the network, closing the lines would mean losing 9,000 miles of superbly engineered rights of way which could be put to better use. These railway tracks overlaid a network of rural roads that were little better than tarmacked cow trails. The government spent vast sums in the 1960s and '70s on new, wider roads and by-passes, but had these permanent ways been converted to bus-ways, for example, express coaches could have replaced trains, providing public transport

48

at a fraction of the cost. A number of bus-ways have been built since, but they have proved costly as they have had to be engineered and built from scratch.

Lloyd's innovative idea led to the formation of the Railway Conversation League, but the concept never really gained an audience in the 1950s or '60s. By the 1970s, it was too late; the closed lines had already, on the whole, been dug up, bridges removed and sections of land sold off for homes and industry.

As for Marples, he went on to greater things, notably a redacted appearance in the Denning Report (he admitted having been familiar with one of the ladies Denning interviewed) and a final hurried escape, twelve years later, from the tax authorities. He had apparently been stashing money away, all those years, in Liechtenstein. He died, unabashed, in his château in Burgundy.

Profumo: Let Scandal Commence

Members of the so-called Establishment continued to perpetuate the myth that they were uncompromisingly pure and blessed with Victorian probity. However, for what seemed like months on end during the spring and summer of 1963, the British public were treated to revelations about the sex lives of individuals that debunked such fantasies for good.

While the Profumo Affair may have threatened national security, that wasn't what sold newspapers. To imagine the mixture of shock and glee with which the story was received, we have to remember that, while people in government had been merrily paying for sex and committing adultery since the Roman times, in 1963 much of Middle England was still culturally located in the puritan, uptight 1950s; indeed, they would probably have seen eye to eye with Gladstone. British culture associated sex with filth (the judge in the Argyll case had found the evidence 'disgusting'); divorced women were tainted; the contraceptive pill was unknown and thus all possible outcomes of unmarried intercourse were concealed; and homosexuality was a criminal offence. The British were prejudiced, anxious, disapproving and ungenerous – but also seething with prurient curiosity. Interest in the *Lady Chatterley* trial in 1960, and in the book itself, had been fuelled by lubricious reports in the popular press.

Jack Profumo, 48, was Secretary of State for War. The first public hint that he had had a fling with a girl called Christine Keeler, thereby possibly endangering national security, was voiced on 21 March in the House of Commons. Labour MP George Wigg wanted to know when 'a government minister' whose conduct was the subject of rumour was going to admit or deny the truth of these rumours. Under cover of Parliamentary privilege, discussion ranged widely, and Profumo's name was spoken aloud.

Wigg's query specifically came down to why Christine Keeler, who appeared to be a prostitute who had been shot at before Christmas in a mews house in Marylebone, had failed to appear at the Old Bailey to bear witness against her alleged assailant. By implication, Profumo had his own reasons for keeping her out of the way, and had made sure she was packed off somewhere.

Jack Profumo had served in North Africa and Italy during the war, had become a brigadier, had been Mentioned in Despatches, and in 1945 had been chief of staff at the British Military Mission in Japan. For the past thirteen years he had given devoted service to his constituents in Stratford-upon-Avon. He was married with children.

The story was nearly two years old. On a warm day in June 1961, while weekending at Cliveden, Lord Astor's home in Buckinghamshire, he had met Christine Keeler. She was a tall brunette with a good figure and haughty cheekbones who wandered through the grounds to Cliveden's inviting swimming pool, where guests were gathered. She was not turned away. She and Profumo knew one another slightly, having met before at Murray's Club in Beak Street.

She was spending that particular weekend in a cottage on the Cliveden Estate, with her friend Stephen Ward and Ward's friend Eugene Ivanov, an assistant naval attaché at the Russian Embassy.

During the week she lived in Marylebone, where she had a room in a flat rented by Stephen Ward (the lynchpin of the whole story in ways which will become apparent). Stephen Ward's own landlord, Peter Rachman, was the freeholder. Rachman was a slum landlord who had looked after Miss Keeler for more than a year. After his meetings with Keeler, he went home every night to his young wife in an expensive house in Hampstead. When matrimony became dull (it didn't take long) he began seeing Keeler's pretty blonde friend, Mandy Rice-Davies.

Keeler and Profumo began an affair that may have ended sometime in the autumn of 1961. It is all rather hazy and depends whose word you trust; Rice-Davies and Keeler later wrote autobiographies that would have it that an entire circle of friends, including Roger Hollis of MI5, Anthony Blunt, Ayub Khan, Profumo and other prominent men, attended sex parties given by Maria Novotny in the winter of 1961/62 and a good time was had by all.

Keeler's on-off boyfriend and minder was occasional jazz musician Lucky Gordon; and in the summer of 1962, Johnny Edgecombe. Both were post-war immigrants from the Caribbean who hung out in Soho and Notting Hill, smoked a little weed, drank a little hooch and generally wouldn't be asked to house parties like the one at Cliveden. Edgecombe had a criminal record. The connection, of course, was Peter Rachman.

Gordon and Edgecombe disliked one another. Both were possessive of Keeler, who, in the second half of 1962, soon after she had met him, told Edgecombe that Lucky Gordon beat her up. Edgecombe went to a Soho club, confronted Gordon and slashed his face so that he required seventeen stitches. Keeler was furious and said she would tell the police who had done it. Edgecombe did not react well and she fled to Stephen Ward's flat, where her old room was now occupied by Mandy Rice-Davies. Edgecombe guessed where she was, got a gun and went there in a cab. She refused to open the door so he shot at it, upon which the police were called.

In January, Johnny Edgecombe ended up at the Old Bailey on a charge of attempting to murder Christine Keeler, who was nowhere to be found; she had gone to Spain and declined to return.

MI5, while they knew that Ivanov and Stephen Ward existed and that Ward knew Profumo and Keeler, claimed to have known nothing about Christine Keeler's affair with Profumo until 28 January. At this point, presumably, they found out what Edgecombe was alleging about Keeler's relationship with Profumo. Certainly, one of their agents reported on 4 February (in the quaint language of that service) that 'The courtesan, Christine Keeler, has told source [a journalist] that she had no intention of putting her name to anything that would embarrass Mr Profumo'. People started to talk.

Two months later, on 21 March, George Wigg stood up in the House and asked a question that provoked a lively debate, with Barbara Castle and Richard Crossman contributing. Had somebody wanted to get Keeler out of the way because Edgecombe was threatening to have his lawyers ask questions in court that might associate Profumo with a sordid circle of people? And if Profumo, Secretary of Sate for War, had been sleeping with Keeler, what about Stephen Ward's friend Ivanov, now back in Moscow, with whom Christine Keeler had been more than friendly at the same time? The implication was that pillow talk probably passed from Profumo to Ivanov through Keeler.

The following day, in a statement to the house, Profumo vehemently denied intimacy with Keeler, assisting with the disappearance of a witness, or causing any possible breach of security. He wrote to the prime minister saying he had never had anything but a perfunctory acquaintance with the woman in question. He had a standing invitation to visit Stephen Ward and sometimes, when he happened to drop by, Christine Keeler was there with other people. He had seen Ivanov on only a few of occasions, one of them an official function.

Macmillan, to whom this gossip was all completely new (and if true, horrifying), was deeply concerned. He confronted Profumo with a letter. It was a note from Profumo to Christine Keeler, dated August 1961, regretting that he would have to be away for a while and asking her to look after herself in his absence. 'Darling,' it began. It was a tender letter, but Profumo dismissed it. He called all his friends 'Darling' and there was nothing in it at all.

Macmillan was convinced that Profumo was telling the truth and he confidently declared as much to the House. In April, Profumo began proceedings against a magazine abroad which saw things differently. And there the matter rested, for a while.

But what of Ward and Ivanov? Stephen Ward was about 50 years old, well connected, amusing and well liked. (He also turned out to be garrulous, self-aggrandising and over-excitable.) Ward had a pre-war American qualification in osteopathy, one of the healing arts that at the time was unrecognised in Britain, although he had served as a captain in the Royal Army Medical Corps in India during the war and apparently treated Gandhi.

Back in London in 1949, he married a fashion model. They separated and she went to live in America. By the early 1960s, he was a well-regarded society osteopath and a court portraitist. Ward also happened to be related to Sir Godfrey Nicholson MP, and in 1961 it was Sir Godfrey who put him in touch with someone at the Foreign Office (FO) to whom both Ward and Sir Godfrey could be useful, occasionally. Both got about socially and, in particular, met many Russians.

That was where things had stood, in the summer of 1961, when someone else (who talked to MI5) noticed that Stephen Ward was trying to ingratiate himself with Eugene Ivanov by boasting of the influential people he knew. Ivanov was a Soviet spy, but was not well suited to the job; he got drunk, made passes at women, and generally made a nuisance of himself, and there had been talk of having a word with the Russians to get him sent home. He had already been arrested for drunkenness on a previous posting in Norway. But now he seemed to be hanging around with Stephen Ward.

MI5 made enquiries and Special Branch directed them to a man who, when called in, said 'that there must have been some mistake since he had never met a Russian in his life ... He was at present engaged in writing a history of the Durham Light Infantry. He was not, and never had been, an osteopath.' This other Stephen Ward was offered a cup of coffee and sent on his way.

They started again, found the right man, and came up with hearsay: he lived in a flat at 17 Wimpole Mews; he had apparently been bankrupt at some point; and he was said to supply, or to have supplied, call girls.

A member of MI5 had a little chat with Ward, who 'was completely open about his association with Ivanov'. Ward boasted 'Eugene ... met Jack Profumo with me socially and on another occasion he met Princess Margaret.' The MI5 man's conclusion was that, 'Despite the fact that some of his political ideas are certainly peculiar and are exploitable by the Russians, I do not think that he is of security interest.' And yet, what is the reader to make of political ideas described as 'peculiar'?

The MI5 man did wonder, however, about the call girls. Ward had introduced him to a girl who 'was obviously sharing the house with him. She was heavily painted and considerably overdressed and I wondered ... whether this is corroborating evidence of the allegation ... that he has been involved in the call-girl racket.' 'Heavily painted and considerably overdressed': it is the voice of the 1890s. Perhaps it reveals a lot about the culture within MI5 at the time. In 1963, Keeler's heavy, black eye-makeup was edgily fashionable.

Anyhow, MI5 enquired no further. Their reasoning was that Ward's possible activities as a pimp appeared to have no relevance to national security. People's private lives were none of their business. What the Service was far more interested in was Ward's observations of Ivanov.

In July of 1961, and fresh from the famous Cliveden house party weekend, Ward could hardly contain himself. Keeler and Ivanov, he gossiped, had knocked back a couple of bottles of whisky at Cliveden together. Profumo had been there at the time.

MI5 asked Sir Norman Brooke, the Cabinet secretary, to have a word. Brooke explained to Profumo that it would be better if he saw no more of Stephen Ward, who was indiscreet and far too friendly with Ivanov. There is no record that either MI5 or Norman Brooke suspected Profumo of having an affair with Keeler, but Profumo got understandably nervous and thought they must suspect something, so the affair cooled for a while. Around this time, at the beginning of August 1961, he sent Keeler the affectionate letter; and later that autumn the affair seems to have petered out.

By May of 1962, though, Ward was still meeting MI5 for cosy little chats. He surprised them by a casual mention of his service, and Sir Godfrey Nicholson's, in passing 'off-the-record' information from the Foreign Office (where Lord Home was Foreign Secretary) to Eugene Ivanov, who presumably would trot off with it to his masters.

Could it be true that the FO was using Ward? MI5 checked and, indeed, it was. Appalled, they pointed out to the Foreign Office that Ward was 'both naïve and indiscreet'. Whether this implied slur on their competence offended someone at the FO so much that they dismissed it in defiance is unknown, but for whatever reason they took no notice and Ward was closer than ever to Ivanov by October 1962 during the Cuban Missile Crisis.

The crisis was a stand-off between Kennedy and Khrushchev. The Soviet Union had begun to construct missile launch sites in Cuba, which was rather too close to Florida for comfort. The USA already had launchpads of its own in Italy, Turkey and the United Kingdom for 'intermediate range' ballistic missiles that would reach Russian cities. Kennedy issued an ultimatum: these Soviet missile sites must be removed or there would be consequences.

For about forty-eight hours the world held its breath in anticipation of Armageddon. The popular imagination across the Northern Hemisphere dreaded a first strike, a retaliation, and then war to the death. Whole populations could be vaporised, as they had been at Nagasaki and Hiroshima.

The Cuban Missile Crisis was the first test of the mutually assured destruction (MAD) strategy that had prevailed for some years. It relied on deterrence to produce peace; and that time, it worked.

Ward, indiscreet as ever, later discussed his role at this time with someone who recounted the conversation to MI5:

Ward says that at the height of the Cuban missile crisis ... Ivanov brought another Russian official, [Vitalij] Loginov [Chargé d'affaires] to see Ward: 'We had practically a Cabinet meeting one night. That was the night when Kennedy made his famous speech on the radio [revealing the existence of the Cuban missile bases] ...' Ivanov, he said, had come to him because he knew that Ward would be able to put information through to the Prime Minister: 'You should have seen what happened. Eugene rang me up in a very worried state and later brought round this man Loginov. Certain messages they gave me they wanted to go to the Foreign Office. The Prime Minister was informed. It had quite a bearing on what transpired later.'

It was true that on 24 October 1962, at one of the tensest moments of the crisis, Ward had passed a message from Ivanov 'that the Soviet Government looked to the United Kingdom as their one hope of conciliation'. When this reached Moscow, the British Ambassador was 'sceptical about both the information and the initiative'. In other words, he judged the source unreliable and the message unbelievable.

On 27 October, Ward accompanied Ivanov to the home of a Foreign Office official, the Earl of Arran, in order 'to get a message to the British Government by indirect means asking them to call a Summit conference in London forthwith'. Lord Arran passed on the message to No. 10 as well as to the Foreign Office. The next day, however, Khrushchev agreed to remove the missile bases from Cuba and the crisis was resolved.

It seems that, in 1961, MI5 had been looking at Ivanov, and looking at Ward, and had deliberately ignored the possible Profumo-Keeler connection because it was not within its remit to investigate sexual scandal unless there was a threat to national security; it concluded, for reasons which remain unclear, that there was not. Macmillan – who had never felt completely at ease with Roger Hollis, preferring to talk to Dick White – was therefore left, in March 1963, to make a fool of himself.

4

APRIL – Ban the Bomb

Polaris and the Nassau Agreement

While the Macmillan government had, since the late 1950s, sought to maintain the illusion of British power by insisting that Britain was able to develop and maintain an independent nuclear deterrent, the US was already moving forward with a new nuclear missile delivery system called Polaris. This replaced an earlier American plan to create a submarine-based missile force modelled on a surfaced submarine carrying four Jupiter missiles, which could be carried and launched horizontally.

The US navy initially favoured a Cruise missile system, but its early launch system meant it had to come up from the depths and stay on the surface before take-off. Submarines were particularly vulnerable to attack during launch and a fully fuelled missile on deck was a sitting target for a Soviet air attack; and rough weather would make the whole process highly unreliable.

Polaris had a lot going for it: rough conditions at sea barely affected the launch, which could be made from a submarine safely underwater and out of sight; and solid-fuelled ballistic missiles also had advantages over cruise missiles in range and accuracy.

The first version of the missile, the Polaris A1, could hit a target 1,000 nautical miles away. The USS *George Washington*, the first ballistic missile submarine, carried sixteen missiles. On 6 May 1962, the first and only time the Americans tested a live strategic nuclear missile, they fired a Polaris with a live W47 warhead in the Pacific. It worked well, and persuaded the US navy that the new Polaris system was best. It persuaded the Royal Navy as well, but Macmillan rejected it.

Macmillan already knew Britain's ageing fleet of Vulcan bombers would be incapable of delivering an effective nuclear attack on the Soviet Union. His defence secretary, Duncan Sandys, had therefore established a new policy of delivering such weapons not by plane, but via guided missiles. This led to substantial sums of money being spent on an ill-fated project called Blue Streak. Around £60 million had been spent in less than two years before Sandys' successor, Harold Watkinson, was forced to cancel the project. In an effort to retrieve some small measure of credibility, the government resolved in March 1960 to buy the American missile system Skybolt.

Just when Macmillan thought he had finally resolved the issue of nuclear defence, President Kennedy announced in December 1962 that the US was cancelling Skybolt due to irremediable technical problems. Macmillan, determined to retain at least the appearance of an independent deterrent, now set out to obtain Polaris, which he had previously rejected and which the Americans were not now minded to supply for fear of alienating France and Germany.

Macmillan and Kennedy, therefore, met in the Bahamas in December 1962 to find a way out of the impasse. Macmillan, a wily operator, first tried the ploy that had always worked with Eisenhower. He later recalled his opening gambit with Kennedy:

I was one of the few who could remember the early days of nuclear weapons. The project, then known as 'Tube Alloys', had been developed originally by British scientists. It was on grounds of safety as well as convenience that Churchill had agreed with Roosevelt that further development should be joint and carried out in the United States. But European countries knew perfectly well that Britain had been first in the field and might be said, up to the end of the War, to be to have had an equal share in the equity with America. After the war, Anglo-American co-operation, which had not previously been covered by any precise or binding legal agreements, was stopped by the McMahon Act, certain clauses of which President Eisenhower had told me frankly were dishonourable.

The McMahon Act had been passed in the wake of Soviet espionage and spy scandals in America, and had sought to restrict American co-operation with other nations, even allies, on defence and other sensitive matters. When the old pals act failed to do the trick, Macmillan changed tack. He claimed that Eisenhower had assured him that, if necessary, Britain could rely upon the US to obtain Polaris, and that should the Americans now seek to use the failure of Skybolt as a 'method of forcing Britain out of an independent nuclear capacity', then the results would be very serious indeed. If Britain was to continue with its 'worldwide commitments', it needed to have some independent nuclear force.

Macmillan's sudden intransigence, and his hint that Britain's willingness to uphold its international commitments was somehow linked to the nuclear issue, led Kennedy and his negotiators to reconsider. They first backtracked on Skybolt. They might, they said, now be minded to supply it after all if Britain paid 50 per cent of the on-going costs. Macmillan artfully pointed out that '[although] the proposed British marriage with Skybolt was not exactly a shotgun wedding, the virginity of the lady must now be regarded as doubtful'.

The following day, Kennedy introduced the concept of a 'multilateral nuclear force'. This proposal initially involved multinational crews and centred on the idea of pooling nuclear forces. Kennedy saw it as a way of avoiding French and German resentment of any nuclear deal between America and Britain. While Macmillan was privately cynical about this idea, describing it in his memoirs as something the Americans 'fondly believed would be attractive to their NATO allies', he seized on it as a face-saving way out.

The result was the Nassau Agreement, under which the United States would supply Britain with Polaris while Britain would manufacture her own warheads. In return, Britain would assign her nuclear fleet to NATO, except in cases where the British government might decide that supreme national interests were at stake.

The official text of the agreement described a meeting that had been courteous, cautious and diplomatic, and with results that were not to Britain's immediate advantage, but it was not released at the time. Macmillan had agreed to Kennedy's proposal to supply five submarines with sixteen missiles each, which would be a massive financial burden. The Minister of Defence, Peter Thorneycroft, who had recently replaced Harold Watkinson, declined to give any figures when questioned in the House of Commons, but estimates of the cost were published together with actual contractual details for the vessels so far completed. The average figure for the 410ft submarines worked out at about $160 million (£57 million), with a single loading of sixteen Polaris A2 missiles. There was no reason to suppose that a British ship of comparable size would be significantly different in price.

No figures were published, either, for the number of missile-firing submarines which the Royal Navy hoped to acquire; indeed, it had probably not yet been decided. Neither was the public told how many missiles each was to carry. Unofficial estimates ranged from 'five ships' to 'ten or twelve'. There had been a great deal of unofficial talk about mini-submarines carrying one or two Polaris missiles each, and also of a larger vessel carrying eight missiles. Most observers, however, believed that the British ships would closely follow the design of the US Ethan Allen class, with sixteen Polaris missiles each. A dozen submarines of this calibre would cost more than £600 million.

A possible clue to the size of the new undersea force was given by Peter Thorneycroft in the House of Commons when he said:

> Taken overall, the Polaris system will not cost us any more than the Skybolt system would have cost ... We could have had the air-launched weapon for £35.7 million plus the purchase costs of the missiles: such a deal was offered by President Kennedy during his initial talk with Mr Macmillan.

In light of such scanty information, Labour's Denis Healy made mischief by speculating on the implications of what Thorneycroft had said. Most of the work of converting the Vulcan B2 force to take Skybolt had already been completed at a cost of just under £15 million, and the bulk of the order for all-British warheads for Skybolt had already been fulfilled. If the Polaris deal was going to be no more expensive, the Royal Navy was hardly going to get more than two ships at the most.

The Polaris Sales Agreement was signed on 6 April 1963 and bristled with acronyms. The UK agreed to assign control over their Polaris missile targeting to the Supreme Allied Commander, Europe (always an

American), providing that in a national emergency when unsupported by the NATO allies, the targeting, permission to fire, and firing of those Polaris missiles would reside with the British authorities. Despite this, the prime minister's consent is and always has been required for deployment of British nuclear weapons.

That was clear enough, but confusingly, operational control of Polaris submarines was assigned to the NATO Supreme Allied Commander, Atlantic, based near Norfolk, Virginia; and the holder of that office routinely delegated that control to the Deputy Commander, Eastern Atlantic, who was always a British admiral.

Polaris was the largest project in the Royal Navy's peacetime history. Although in 1964 the incoming Labour government considered cancelling it and converting the submarines into conventionally armed vessels, Wilson himself later admitted that production of Polaris missiles was 'well past the point of no return; there could be no question of cancelling them, except at inordinate cost'. So it went ahead, as part of NATO defences: 'There was to be no nuclear pretence or suggestion of a go-it-alone British nuclear war against the Soviet Union.'

Wilson also recognised that Polaris gave Britain a global nuclear capacity for £150 million less than a V bomber force would have cost. By adopting many American methodologies and components, Polaris was finished on time and within budget, which was highly unusual for a British military project. The first one was tested in 1968.

In the end, Kennedy's aim to create a multilateral nuclear force was scuppered not by Macmillan, who had arguably paid lip-service to the idea to get Kennedy to sign the agreement. It was de Gaulle's refusal to play the game which eventually torpedoed the multinational force: 'We don't like the idea,' said the French 'and can't afford the high cost.'

American defence experts had to concede that without the French, there could be no claim that Polaris was in any sense a 'multinational' defence. The idea was, therefore, conveniently referred to a committee for further study and no more was heard of it.

Lord Home, the Foreign Secretary, and Peter Thorneycroft, the Defence Minister, who, like Macmillan, privately opposed the scheme from the start, were greatly relieved. De Gaulle insisted, in the words of his spokesman, that 'There is not the slightest chance that France will put her nuclear weapons under control of NATO in the foreseeable future.'

He never liked having Americans in his backyard, but they needed him if NATO was to have any credibility. Accordingly, France was offered a share in control of 175 British H-bombers and three US Polaris submarines, which gave it a permanent seat on the NATO nuclear executive. De Gaulle also agreed that French squadrons would take a couple of atom bombs already allotted to NATO and based in Germany.

British (and American) faces were saved all round, but only just.

The Committee of 100

The signing of the Polaris Sales Agreement sparked renewed protests by the Campaign for Nuclear Disarmament (CND), particularly from among its more militant supporters, known as 'The Committee of 100'. The Committee, whose members believed in mass, non-violent, civil disobedience, was set up in 1960 by 100 signatories that included Bertrand Russell, Ralph Schoenman, Canon Michael Collins and Ralph Miliband (father of Ed and David). At its founding meeting on 22 October 1960, Lord Russell was elected as president and Michael Randle as secretary. Bertrand Russell wrote an article for the *New Statesman* in February, in which he expounded the Committee's purpose and objectives:

> There is a very widespread feeling that however bad their (*the Government's*) policies may be, there is nothing that private people can do about it. This is a complete mistake. If all those who disapprove of government policy were to join massive demonstrations of civil disobedience they could render government folly impossible and compel the so-called statesmen to acquiesce in measures that would make human survival possible. Such a vast movement, inspired by outraged public opinion is possible, perhaps it is imminent. If you join it you will be doing something important to preserve your family, compatriots and the world.

The Committee proceeded to organise sit-down demonstrations for which they sought a minimum of 2,000 volunteers, who would pledge to take part. The first such protest took place outside the Ministry of Defence; well over 2,000 people took part, the police kept their distance and there were no arrests. At the next sit-down protest in Parliament

Square, the police decided to move in and arrested 826 protesters. By the spring of 1963, support for the sit-ins seemed to be dwindling. While their early protests had attracted considerable numbers, it was noted within CND and in the press that few of the founding 100 members personally took part in these protests.

The Committee clearly hoped that the renewed controversy surrounding Britain's nuclear deterrent would galvanise their fortunes. A mass march down Whitehall was, therefore, planned on 14 April in defiance of the police. According to the *Daily Express*:

> 14,000 copies of extracts from the 'Spies for Peace' pamphlet on secret government plans to withstand a nuclear attack are being distributed to the marchers by the Committee of 100. To meet the Whitehall invasion planned by the breakaway section of the nuclear disarmers, 700 police are ready to move up as required. Coaches and lorries will be waiting to move demonstrators who have to be forcibly lifted from Whitehall, Parliament Square, or any of the 36 streets which the police will close from midday until midnight.

The move on Whitehall was announced on 13 April by a spokesman for The Committee of 100. About 15,000 marchers had bedded down at Chiswick by nightfall and the main CND contingent was expected to proceed to Hyde Park. Peter Cadogan, the spokesman for The Committee of 100, said the Hyde Park rally would be an anti-climax and Committee members planned to stage a 'more emphatic' demonstration. Special Branch apparently had information to suggest that 2,000 supporters of the Committee planned to force their way into Whitehall.

Police Commissioner Sir Joseph Simpson sent officers to warn the marchers that they were liable to be arrested if they disobeyed police orders, in streets stretching from Marble Arch to Charing Cross. The night before the demonstration, Committee members were busy at a secret headquarters in London turning out extracts from the 'Spies for Peace' pamphlet, revealing the secret underground sites of twelve area administrative centres, which would operate in wartime. However, in an interview with the *Daily Express*, Cadogan was more reticent: 'I do not know who wrote the abbreviated version. All I know is that 14,000 copies are being distributed.'

Cadogan, a 42-year-old Cambridge teacher, took part in the main march from Aldermaston. He denied 'having anything to do with the revelation of the secrets' and added, 'Now that the information has been made public I regard it as our duty to tell the people as much as we can about these secret places.'

Despite the renewed Polaris controversy, the protest of 14 April failed to reignite the Committee's earlier momentum. It would be another two decades before the issue of nuclear weapons would again raise its head as a major political issue.

5

MAY – It's all in the Game

A man for all seasons

On 1 August 1962, the England football manager, Walter Winterbottom, who had held the post since 1946, announced that he was resigning to become general secretary of the Central Council of Physical Recreation. The Football Association had met to consider a replacement and the overwhelming consensus was that Winterbottom's assistant, Jimmy Adamson of Burnley, was the best man for the job. Indeed, the press had for some time dubbed Burnley 'the team of the '60s' and forecast that they would dominate the domestic game for the next ten years in the same way that Wolves had dominated the previous decade.

However, the FA were in for a shock, for two days before England's next game on 3 October against France, Adamson dramatically announced that he would not be accepting the job after all. Apparently, his family was unhappy about having to move south to London and after some weeks of soul-searching, he decided to stay with Burnley.

The former Wolves and England forward Dennis Wilshaw (a senior FA coach) was apparently sounded out unofficially soon after Adamson's announcement, but he too declined. While they briefly toyed with the idea of a panel of league mangers to replace Winterbottom, the FA quickly resolved to advertise the post and received fifty-nine applications. While there is no record in the FA archives as to the identity of the other fifty-eight, an application was received from Alf Ramsey, the former Spurs and England defender who was currently manager of Ipswich Town. Ramsey had, in a period of four years, won promotion for Ipswich from the Third to the First Division, where they won the League Championship in their first season in the top flight.

Ramsey was duly offered the job and the announcement that he was to be appointed was made by the FA on 25 October. Ramsey's club were reluctant to release him before the end of the season and it was, therefore, agreed that he would take over the post on a full-time basis on 1 May 1963. He would, however, have a part-time involvement in the meantime and be part of the panel of selectors who would choose the team for the next three fixtures prior to 1 May. At a press conference convened to announce his appointment, a decidedly uncomfortable Ramsey had told the assembled journalists that 'England will win the World Cup in 1966'. Most of those present either took Ramsey to be an incurable optimistic or a man suffering from self-delusion.

Just before Christmas, the FA announced that his first official game as manager, with sole responsibility for team selection, would be against world champions Brazil at Wembley on 8 May. Although England had comfortably beat Wales on 21 November, they played poorly against France and Scotland, losing both games. There was, therefore, a great deal at stake and the Brazilians were hardly the opponents of choice for any incoming manager.

In the match-day programme, Ramsey spoke exclusively to John Graydon, the editor of *Sports World*. When Graydon asked him what his overall policy would be as manager of England, Ramsey unhesitatingly replied: 'I must have in the England team men who want to play for their country and are prepared to put in an all-out effort. There can be no compromise.'

He also laid emphasis on the philosophy that would later be seen as his key to success: 'Let's face the fact that we must have in the England team the splendid club spirit I experienced when I stepped into the side in the days of Frank Swift, Billy Wright, Tom Finney and Stanley

Matthews ... for me, one of the most important thing is for our players to really get to know each other as footballers and men.' Ramsey's first team selection as full-time manager (see Appendix 1) was pitted against a Brazilian team that, although experimenting with new players, still had as its backbone a good many of the stars that had graced the previous year's World Cup final. Indeed, England had lost 3-1 to the Brazilians in the quarter-final.

Ramsey had initially announced that Everton midfielder Tony Kay would make his England debut against Brazil. Kay, who had become Britain's most expensive player the previous year when Everton paid Sheffield Wednesday £60,000 to sign him, was tipped by the press to be one of the key players on whom England's 1966 World Cup hopes would hang. He was, however, withdrawn shortly before the game by Everton and Ramsey drafted in Liverpool's Gordon Milne to replace him. Kay eventually played his first (and last) game for England against Switzerland four weeks later, before being banned for life by the FA for match fixing (in December 1962 he had placed a bet that Wednesday would lose against Ipswich Town shortly before his transfer to Everton).

In front of a 93,000 crowd, England dominated long periods of play, but the forward line lacked the imagination and opportunity to capitalise on the opportunities that came their way. The Brazilians, in contrast, took the lead mid-way through the first half when Pepe scored from a 25 yd banana-kick, which lured Banks away from the far post and sailed into the top corner of the net. England, who played a standard game of passing the ball up the field in the hope that one of the wingers would get in a lucky cross, looked like losing the game until two minutes from the end. A low shot into the penalty area by Jimmy Armfield was quickly flicked on by Bobby Charlton and passed into the net by Brian Douglas. Ramsey had come through the ordeal with a degree satisfaction, even though England's 'old hat' tactics were clearly still out of step with those being employed by first-class opposition.

'We are the Champions!'

Because of the record number of postponed games during the winter months, the domestic football season did not end until Saturday 18 May. When the whistle blew at 4.50 p.m., Everton were crowned

First Division champions for the first time since the Second World War, with a star-studded team that earned them the tag of 'Cheque Book Champions' in the press. They had lost only six games out of forty-two, with strikers Alex Young and Roy Vernon scoring forty-six goals between them. The team, assembled by manager Harry Catterick, was valued at over £400,000, an eye-watering sum in those days. In addition to Vernon and Young, it included star signings such as Billy Bingham, Jimmy Gabriel, Derek Temple, Bobby Collins and Brian Labone.

By contrast, Stoke City's new manager Tony Waddington had assembled a team of bargain basement stars in the twilight of their careers and blended them in with a crop of promising youngsters. His biggest bargain had been secured eighteen months previously when he had bought 46-year-old Stanley Matthews from Blackpool for £3,500. Stoke City, languishing in the Second Division at the time, immediately saw their home gates rise from an average of 8,000 to well over 30,000. Matthews' very presence seemed to galvanise his teammates who, by the last home game of the 1962/63 season against Luton Town, were just two points away from promotion back to the First Division. Before a gate of 34,000 fans, Matthews scored the second of two Stoke goals to clinch the Championship.

While Manchester United, despite fielding nine international players, was lucky not to be relegated to the Second Division, they succeeded in reaching the FA Cup final on 25 May against Leicester City. Shown live on the BBC's *Cup Final Grandstand*, the broadcasters had asked the FA if one of the teams could change to a white strip for the final. Although United wore red shirts and City blue, on black and white television they would be virtually indistinguishable. The FA agreed and Leicester, who lost the toss, was given the white kits.

During the opening quarter of an hour, United struggled to find their feet, during which time Leicester were unlucky not to be 3-0 up. Having survived the opening setbacks, United went on to take a grip of the game and won by a margin of 3-1. It was their first trophy since the Munich air disaster of 1958 and would herald a run of success that would culminate in achieving manager Matt Busby's dream of winning the European Cup in 1968.

United were not, however, the first English team to win a European trophy. That honour went to Tottenham Hotspur.

European Champions

Tottenham Hotspur had narrowly failed to reach the final of the 1962 European Cup competition, losing 4-3 on aggregate to Benfica in the semi-final. The game had been fuelled with controversy due to two Spurs goals being disallowed. They had, however, qualified for the European Cup Winners' Cup by retaining the FA Cup in 1962 by defeating a highly fancied Burnley team at Wembley. Their journey to the Cup Winners' Cup final began with a first round clash against Scottish Cup winners Rangers, which the press had dubbed 'The Battle of Britain' in the run up to first leg at White Hart Lane.

Midfielder John White had opened the scoring from a Jimmy Greaves corner after only four minutes, although Rangers struck back and equalised within five minutes. Another Greaves corner enabled White to head his second, before centre-forward Les Allen made it three. Under pressure, the Rangers defence conceded an own goal, but almost immediately managed to score a second. Ten minutes from the full time, another Greaves corner saw Maurice Norman score the fifth and final goal, which was to them a decisive advantage in front of 80,000 Rangers fans for the second leg at Ibrox Park. Goals from Jimmy Greaves and Bobby Smith gave Spurs an 8-4 aggregate victory.

In the first leg of the second round, Spurs were out-classed and out-played by Slovan Bratislava. With a number of injuries and an excessively muddy pitch, Spurs found themselves struggling from the start and were lucky not to lose by more than the 2-0 final score. In the second leg, with a full-strength team and a home crowd, they were transformed and won the game 6-0 with two goals from Jimmy Greaves and one apiece from Dave Mackay, Bobby Smith, John White and Cliff Jones.

Spurs were now only one game away from the final and played OFK Belgrade in the semi-final, winning the first leg 2-1 with goals from John White and Terry Dyson. Again, they had come through despite having to play with ten men after Jimmy Greaves had been sent off. In the second leg, captain Danny Blanchflower returned after injury, although Greaves was unable to play due to being suspended after the first leg.

Spurs took the lead after half an hour, only for OFK to equalise six minutes later. A pass from Dave Mackay two minutes before half time set up Terry Dyson to score Spurs' second. During the second half, OFK fought back and came close to scoring on several occasions. Spurs survived the onslaught and Bobby Smith finally headed in a third goal to secure Spurs' place in the final.

Held on 15 May at the Feyenoord Stadium in Rotterdam against favourites and holders Athletico Madrid, the game promised to be a landmark match. Spurs' morale was hit shortly before journeying to Holland with Dave Mackay being declared unfit to play due to injury. According to the later recollections of Jimmy Greaves, manager Bill Nicholson was profuse in his praise of the Athletico players in the pre-match pep talk, but Blanchflower piped up and reminded everyone that Spurs had a host of accomplished players who were more than a match for the Spaniards.

Tottenham began the game in an uneasy fashion, but having survived the opening minutes were two goals ahead by half time through Jimmy Greaves and John White. Although a penalty was conceded in the second half, Spurs weathered a series of Athletico attacks for Terry Dyson to score the third Spurs goal. A cross from Dyson led to Greaves making it four. Dyson himself then scored again to make it a 5-1 victory for Spurs. He had scored twice and created two other goals as Spurs became the first British team to win a European trophy.

Greaves recalled that at the end of the game, Bobby Smith had jokingly suggested that Dyson should retire immediately as he would never play as well again. In the semi-final and final, he had scored three goals and created four more. When the trophy was shown to large crowds from the balcony of Haringey Town Hall a day after the final, captain Danny Blanchflower immediately handed it over to Dyson who was acknowledged by all and sundry as the man whose efforts had won the day for Spurs.

It was, however, to be the team's high watermark. It would be a further four years before Spurs won another trophy, by which time Jimmy Greaves would be the only player from the Rotterdam final still wearing a Spurs shirt.

The Headless Man

The Duke of Argyll was suing his duchess for divorce, citing another man. He had originally filed for divorce in 1959 after finding his wife's sexually explicit diaries and some Polaroid photographs, but four years of legal wrangling had prevented the case from coming to court.

The hearing had begun in Edinburgh in March, when the Profumo Affair occupied many column inches in the London dailies. Society divorces, if a third party was cited, always made good gossip-column material, but this one wasn't conveniently at the divorce court end of Fleet Street, and there were distractions that month. Few journalists expected the evidence to be quite as lurid as it was, but by the date in May, when Judge Wheatley gave his final decision based on a four-and-a-half-hour character assassination of the duchess, the public was hungry for more scandal.

The duke and duchess had been married since 1950. He had been divorced twice, and she once, before they met on a blind date, married in haste at Caxton Hall and repented at leisure. Both already had children. The marriage appeared to have broken down within the first three or four years. Although the duke was accusing the duchess of infidelity, it did rather stretch credibility to assume that he had been sitting at home waiting up for her with a cup of cocoa until this final recourse to the divorce court. But the British being what they were, a faithless wife was far more reprehensible (and interesting) than a faithless husband.

For some reason – presumably financial, since the duchess, who had been born into wealth, spent money with abandon – her case was defended; but surely only arrogance could have made her think she might win. The duke's case was devastating. He told the court that in the course of their marriage he could count eighty-eight men with whom she had had affairs; he knew this from her diaries, here produced, and also from four photographs of her lovers *in flagrante*, displayed to the court.

It is hard not to sympathise with the duchess' lawyers. The only defence they came up with was a blow to the head, which apparently had occurred when Margaret (then Mrs Charles Sweeny) fell down a lift shaft in 1943. After this, it was said, she had lost her sense of taste and smell, and had become sexually voracious. But since they could not show that she had been a woman of irreproachable virtue before, the argument lacked force.

The art deco bathroom of the duchess' home at 48 Upper Grosvenor Street, Mayfair, was about to become familiar to millions. All the photographs had been taken there, by the new Polaroid process. One of them showed the duchess performing oral sex on a naked man. She was identifiable by the three-strand pearl necklace she always wore. He was shown from the neck down, so he was called the 'Headless Man' by the press. Another picture was of a man masturbating for the camera in the same bathroom; again it was cropped at the neck.

Rumours flew about the town. People in the know remembered that Margaret, Duchess of Argyll, a regular little goer as no-one would deny, had once known Duncan Sandys, Cabinet minister, very well; and that she'd had a fling with Douglas Fairbanks Junior, the actor. Other prominent men were mentioned, although those are the two that did tend to recur. No names appeared in the press, though.

On 25 May, Lord Wheatley delivered his verdict, in which he minced no words when it came to the duchess:

She is a highly sexed woman who has ceased to be satisfied with normal sexual activities and has started to indulge in disgusting sexual activities to gratify a debased sexual appetite. A completely promiscuous woman whose sexual appetite could only be satisfied by a number of men, whose promiscuity had extended to perversion and whose attitude to the sanctity of marriage was what moderns would call enlightened, but which in plain language was wholly immoral.

Maybe the Edinburgh court hadn't been such a good idea after all. The press were delighted: among the eighty-eight lovers, they reported, had been 'three Cabinet Ministers and two members of the Royal Family'. The court had been told that one of the Cabinet had agreed to have his penis examined in order to prove he was not the 'Headless Man'.

There was no stopping the London papers after this. Rumours almost identified (but didn't quite) various members of the Cabinet and other Establishment figures. One story suggested that 'a Cabinet Minister' had been caught in Richmond Park having oral sex with a prostitute. Another involved eight High Court judges at an orgy. 'One, perhaps,' Macmillan is supposed to have said, 'two conceivably. But eight – I just can't believe it.'

He had some nasty surprises to come.

James Bond crosses the Atlantic

Even before the first James Bond film, *Dr No*, had been completed in 1962, United Artists began a marketing campaign to make James Bond a well-known name in America. Bond creator Ian Fleming, too, had always set his mind on 007 conquering the United States. Indeed, not long after his first book, *Casino Royale*, was published in America in 1954, Fleming had persuaded CBS to make a pilot television episode for a possible series of James Bond short stories. However, CBS scriptwriters reversed the characters of Bond and Felix Leiter so that Bond was American and Leiter English, much to Fleming's chagrin. While the pilot was generally considered to be a competent production, CBS decided against taking up the option to make a series. It would be over six years before Fleming could persuade another company to look again at the screen potential of Bond.

The desire to promote Bond in America was hardly surprising, bearing in mind that the two film producers who had brought the rights to the James Bond books, Harry Saltzman and Albert Broccoli, of Eon Productions, were both Americans, as was the United Artists Corporation.

To begin the US marketing campaign, newspapers and magazines received a set of Bond books, as well as a booklet detailing the Bond character and a picture of Ursula Andress, Sean Connery's co-star in *Dr No*. Eon and United Artists made licencing deals centring on Bond's tastes, having merchandising tie-ins with drink, cigarette and car companies. The campaign also focused on Ian Fleming, who was now belatedly becoming a recognised figure in America. This was due, in no small part, to President Kennedy, who on 17 March 1961 had told *Life Magazine* that *From Russia with Love* was one of his top ten favourite books.

In March 1963, Sean Connery and *Dr No* director Terence Young set off for a nationwide tour of America, which included exclusive screenings of the film for the press and other media, and culminated in a well-publicised event in Kingston, Jamaica, where most of the film was set. From Kingston, Young, Connery, Andress and other cast members proceeded to the North American premiere, which took place on 8 May. *Dr No* was initially shown in 450 cinemas in the Midwest and Southwest regions. On 29 May it opened in both Los Angeles and New York City, screening in eighty-four movie theatres across the city.

While the film received mixed reviews, virtually all acknowledged Sean Connery's charisma as overcoming any flaws of the plot and low-budget production. The film's first American run in 1963 grossed $2 million, which was considered to be highly satisfactory by United

Artists, bearing in mind the film itself had only cost $1 million to make. This increased to $6 million after it was re-released in 1965, as a double feature with *From Russia with Love*.

For Ian Fleming, 1963 would be a year of mixed blessings. With the successful launch in America of *Dr No* and a highly anticipated follow-up, *From Russia with Love*, in the can, the outlook for Fleming looked extremely positive. However, within a few short months, a case in the High Court would not only threaten to ruin him financially, but would call into question his honesty, integrity and whether or not he was really solely responsible for the Bond formula that had made *Dr No* and *From Russia with Love* box office successes.

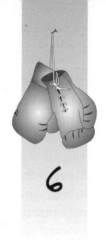

6

JUNE - Scandal

Our 'Enery

Henry Cooper, probably Britain's best-loved boxer, was British and Commonwealth Heavyweight Champion, and had for some time had a claim to fight with a World Boxing Council (WBC) heavyweight contender for the world title. He had, in fact, been offered a fight with the current World Champion, Sonny Liston, when Liston was a contender for Floyd Patterson's title the previous year. However, Cooper's manager, Jim Wicks, retorted: 'I would not allow my 'Enry into the same room as him, let alone the same ring.'

By this he meant that Cooper was more of a technical boxer than Liston; a bear of a man who usually won his fights by knockout during the first or second round. Former World Champion Floyd Patterson had also done his best to avoid a bout with Liston, but had eventually had to succumb to public and British Boxing Board pressure. Liston knocked him out in two minutes and six seconds, the third fasted knockout in boxing history.

In early 1963, Cooper had been offered a bout against 21-year-old Cassius Clay, who was ranked World No. 3 behind Liston and Patterson. The offer was accepted by Wicks and sanctioned by the British Boxing Board of Control to take place at Wembley Stadium on 18 June 1963.

Cooper was born in Lambeth in South London on 3 May 1934 and grew up on the Bellingham council estate in Lewisham. He served his National Service in the Royal Army Ordnance Corps where he was recruited for his boxing ability. He began his boxing career in 1949 as an amateur with the Eltham Amateur Boxing Club, and won seventy-three of eighty-four fights. At the age of 17, he won the first of two Amateur Boxing Association light-heavyweight titles and represented Britain in the 1952 Olympics. Henry and his twin brother, George, turned professional together under the management of Jim Wicks.

He took the British heavyweight title from Brian London in a fifteen-round fight in January 1959, and held the title for ten years before resigning it in protest at the British Boxing Board of Control's refusal to sanction a title fight against World Boxing Association's (WBA) World Heavyweight Champion Jimmy Ellis.

When Cassius Clay came to England to prepare for the bout with Cooper, some newspapers didn't rate him and pointed out that he had beaten only six other boxers since turning professional, and the only one of note was Archie Moore, who, at the age of 46, was old enough to be Clay's father. Cooper and Wicks knew differently and prepared for a tough fight. Basing his training camp at the Fellowship Inn pub in Bellingham, they turned the pub's ballroom into a gymnasium and moved in five weeks before the fight.

Each day, members of the public queued up to come in and watch Cooper train for a charge of sixpence, with all proceeds being donated to pensioners in Bellingham. American boxer Alonzo Johnson was hired as Cooper's sparring partner for $500, his return airfare, and full board and lodgings in Bellingham. Johnson had fought Clay in Louisville, Kentucky and by all accounts was unlucky to lose. Wicks felt that Johnson not only knew Clay's tactics and fighting style inside out, but could imitate them perfectly, ensuring that Cooper would be fully prepared for every eventuality.

The two boxers first came face-to-face on BBC TV's *Sportsview* programme four days before the fight. Apart from shaking hands, the two remained on opposite sides of the studio. Clay, however, lost no opportunity to promote himself. His well-rehearsed act of predicting the round in which he would win and declaring 'I am the Prettiest, I am the Greatest' was hardly original. In fact, the act was lifted almost in its entirety from the American wrestler Gorgeous George. When George went into the ring he wore crown and a purple velvet train held by two girls. He would then run around the ring shouting, 'I am the Greatest, I am the Greatest'.

Clay certainly used the strategy to great effect, and put his prediction for the fight into amusing verse at the fight press conference:

> *My prophecies*, by Cassius Clay:
> When Cassius says a fight will go for five rounds
> The bell for the sixth just never sounds
> When I tangled with Archie I predicted four
> And that's all there was, there wasn't any Moore
> When they queried me about the Cooper bout
> I answered with Shakespearean thrift:
> When they asked me what round I'd knock Henry out
> I answered, Henry the Fifth!

His antics certainly succeeded in selling tickets and helped attract a 50,000-strong crowd, a record for a British boxing bout. The fight itself very nearly derailed Clay's plan to challenge Sonny Liston in his next fight and is a source of argument to this day.

While Clay's mobility, lightning reflexes, height, reach and unorthodox defensive tactic of pulling back from punches made him a frustrating opponent, some of Cooper's work during the opening rounds has been described as 'very near the knuckle', with Clay later complaining of being repeatedly hit on the break. Cooper later recalled that:

> In the first round my problem was to try and get in distance to land my punches. He was a stone and a half heavier than me at the time and he must have the longest reach in the game – between four and five inches longer than mine. From finger-tip to finger-tip he was seventy-nine inches. You feel a man out in the first round, and jabbing away I found I was six inches short.

In the second round, Cooper tried to put pressure on Clay and trap him on the ropes. With Clay's corner shouting out 'stick and move, stick and move', Cooper was doing his best to keep a moving target in front of his opponent. In the third, however, Clay managed to hit Cooper over his weak left eye, badly splitting it. While Wicks wanted to stop the fight there and then, Cooper was determined to fight on. He knew that, with a 2½in cut over his eye, the fourth round was now or never in terms of rescuing the fight. In the dying seconds of the round, Cooper caught Clay with a left hook. While the ropes helped Cooper land the punch, they also saved Clay, whose armpit caught in the ropes going down, preventing his head from hitting the canvas-covered boards, which made up the floor of the ring. Hitting his head on the floor would more than likely have knocked him unconscious.

As Clay slowly hauled himself up from the ropes on a count of five, he was literally saved by the bell. He started slowly towards his trainer, Angelo Dundee, who in the first of three serious infringements of the rules guided him towards the corner and on to his stool. At first Dundee tried talking and slapping Clay's legs. Clay, still groggy, seemed at this point to misunderstand Dundee's instructions and tried to get off the stool. Dundee then used smelling salts – another serious violation of the rules. The only stimulant allowed under BBC rules at the time was water. Thirdly, Dundee also played for time by opening a small tear in one of Clay's gloves and proceeded to tell the referee that he needed a new pair of gloves. Although none were available, the start of round five was delayed.

Cooper started round five aggressively, attempting to make good his advantage, but a recovered Clay effectively countered and Cooper was hit high on the face with a hard right, which opened a severe cut under his eye. Referee Tommy Little was at this point forced to stop the fight and award the bout to Clay, even though Cooper was still ahead on points.

While Cooper had lost the fight, it was judged to be one of his best ever performances. If nothing else, he received the accolade of being the first boxer to knock down the man who would soon be world champion.

'Let them come to Berlin'

By 1963 the infamous Berlin Wall had been in place for two years and had become the living symbol of the Cold War conflict. From the moment of his election as president some thirty months before, John F. Kennedy had sought to place himself at the forefront of the 'cause of freedom'. In June 1963, he undertook a tour of Europe to promote the concept of Atlantic unity.

On 25 June he spoke at the Paulskirche in Frankfurt, where he emphasised America's commitment to Europe:

The United States will risk its cities to defend yours because we need your freedom to protect ours. The choice of paths to the unity of Europe is a choice which Europe must make. Nor do I believe that there is any one right course or any single pattern. It is Europeans who are building Europe.

An articulate and stirring speaker, Kennedy saw Berlin as 'freedom's frontier' and decided to go to the Berlin Wall and lay down a gauntlet to the Russians.

On 26 June 1963, Kennedy gave a speech in West Berlin which many rate as one of his best ever. Sometimes known as the *'Ich bin ein Berliner'* ('I am a Berliner') speech, it was aimed as much at West Berliners as it was the Russians, and was without doubt a clear statement of American intent in the wake of the construction of the Berlin Wall and East Germany's policy of shooting anyone attempting to escape from the East on sight.

The speech was made from a platform erected on the steps of the Rathaus Schöneberg. Accompanying Kennedy was Lucius Clay, the US Administrator of West Germany, US Secretary of State Dean Rusk, West German Chancellor Konrad Adenauer, the Mayor of West Berlin, Willy Brandt, and Otto Bach, President of the German House of Representatives. Bach spoke first about recent developments in Berlin and was followed by Adenauer, who introduced Kennedy.

To an estimated audience of 450,000 people, the president said: 'Two thousand years ago the proudest boast was *Civis Romanus Sum* (I am a Roman Citizen); today, in the world of freedom, the proudest boast is *Ich bin ein Berliner!*'

It is notable that the president was accompanied not by Robert Lochner but by Heinz Weber of the US Berlin Mission. Weber's job was to translate the speech to the audience and it is from him that we get the claim that Kennedy completely disregarded certain parts of the prepared text, which had taken weeks to prepare, and improvised instead. According to Weber, Kennedy says, 'more than he should, something different from what his advisers had recommended, and is more provocative than he had intended to be.'

It is thought that he is referring to the following passage in particular:

There are many people in the world who really don't understand, or say they don't, what is the greatest issue between the free world and the communist world – Let them come to Berlin!

There are some who say that communism is the wave of the future – Let them come to Berlin!

And there are even a few who say that it is true that communism is an evil system, but it permits us to make economic progress.

Lass sie nach Berlin kommen! Let them come to Berlin!

In the words of Kennedy's aide, Arthur Schlesinger, the crowd, estimated to be three-fifths of the population of West Berlin, 'shook itself and roared like an animal'. Kennedy concluded the speech by asserting: 'All free men, wherever they may live, are citizens of Berlin, and, therefore, as a free man, I take pride in the words *"Ich bin ein Berliner"*.'

The speech was, in part, influenced by an earlier speech Kennedy had given at a civic reception on 4 May 1962 in Louisiana. In that speech he used the same phrase *Civis Romanus Sum*, but in a different context:

Two thousand years ago the proudest boast was to say, 'I am a citizen of Rome'. Today, I believe, in 1962 the proudest boast is to say, 'I am a citizen of the United States'.

Before leaving Washington, Kennedy had taken part in practice sessions running through the German quotations in the proposed speech. It soon became clear that he did not have sufficient grasp of the language to quote extended passages and so instead restricted himself to shorter sentences.

There are differing accounts on the origin of the phrase *'Ich bin ein Berliner'*. Kennedy's aide Ted Sorensen claimed in his memoir, *Counselor: A Life at the Edge of History*, that he had played a major role in writing the speech. Robert Lochner, a Berlin interpreter, also claimed in his memoirs that Kennedy had asked him for a translation of 'I am a Berliner', and that they practiced the phrase in Mayor Willy Brandt's office.

While the immediate response from the West German population was positive, the Soviet authorities were less pleased with the combative 'Let them come to Berlin'. Only two weeks previously, Kennedy had spoken in more conciliatory tones, referring to 'improving relations with the Soviet Union'. Khrushchev, in a broadcast on Radio Moscow two days later, remarked that, 'one would think that the speeches were made by two different presidents'.

Profumo: Resignation

By the beginning of June, Profumo must have known the game was up. Lucky Gordon had been arrested and charged with having attacked Christine Keeler, upon her return from Spain, with intent to cause her both actual and grievous bodily harm. His trial in June would be widely publicised and Keeler, summonsed to appear as a witness for a second time, could hardly disappear again. Gordon's counsel would try to diminish the credibility of the chief witness by exposing her private life, which, as Lucky Gordon well knew, had involved the Secretary of State for War as well as the assistant naval attaché at the Russian Embassy.

Then there was Mandy Rice-Davies, who had been arrested when about to board a flight to Spain, charged with possession of a fake driving licence, kept inside on remand and, allegedly, put under pressure by the police to bear witness against Stephen Ward in court.

On 4 June, therefore, Jack Profumo resigned. In his letter to Macmillan he admitted that, on 22 March, when he had made a personal statement to the House denying 'assisting with the disappearance of a witness' and involvement with Christine Keeler, aged 21, which might have led to a 'possible breach of security', he had lied.

On 5 June, the letter and the prime minister's reply, accepting his resignation, were published. 'he lied' screamed the headlines, in bold type.

The *Daily Telegraph* was more interested in the story behind the story, especially the question of national security. Stephen Ward revelled in publicity: he had given a 'my life with Christine' piece to the *Sunday Pictorial* in March, and now he obliged the *Telegraph* with a fulsome interview, which appeared on 6 June. Two years ago, he said, he had informed 'a man in the security service at the War Office' about the Ivanov-Profumo link via a mutual friend, because he had been worried about it, and he had written to Home Secretary Henry Brooke in May this year to say so, too. Ward went on to say that he had even introduced Christine Keeler to the security man. When nothing seemed to be happening, he had even told Commander Townsend of Scotland Yard what the security man's name was. It had all been rather farcical; at some point, the 'security men' watching Ivanov outside 17 Wimpole Mews had 'had an encounter with' the ones watching Profumo.

All he'd done, Stephen Ward protested, was rent a room in his flat to Christine Keeler and, later on, to her friend Mandy; he was not, as Gordon and others had said, running a call girl racket; and life had become a nightmare. All he'd been trying to do, he claimed, was inform the authorities of a possible security risk.

In other quarters, notably American ones, doubts were being cast on the viability and competence of MI5. On 14 June, a potentially controversial lead came from a Western double agent in Soviet intelligence (whose name remains classified). On 14 June, nine days after Profumo's resignation, the agent reported having overheard a Soviet intelligence officer say 'that the Russians had in fact received a lot of useful information from Profumo through Christine Keeler, with whom Ivanov had established contact, and in whose apartment Ivanov had even been able to lay on eavesdropping operations at the appropriate times.' The agent's report did not go to MI5, but to the Americans. J. Edgar Hoover, in charge of the FBI, believed that the British intelligence service 'leaked like a sieve'. He made sure that this report was forwarded straight to US Attorney General Robert Kennedy to pass on to his brother, the president. President Kennedy was due to meet Macmillan in July.

According to MI5 later, although the double agent did not realise it, the Soviet intelligence officer's boast was based on deeply improbable speculation rather than reliable intelligence. The key Russian intelligence agencies were the GRU (for military intelligence) and the KGB (home and abroad). Ivanov was a GRU officer and, in their view, it was highly unlikely that detailed reports on his operations would have been sent to the KGB residency, where the double agent was stationed. Certainly there is no evidence that President Kennedy ever told Macmillan, or even that Robert Kennedy passed the intelligence on. He sometimes did disregard Hoover's advice.

MI5 was not told about the double agent's report until 1966. The press reported, though, that on 15 June, Home Secretary Henry Brooke was suddenly called back to England for unexplained reasons.

There was more. Michael Eddowes, a prominent divorce lawyer and friend of Stephen Ward, gave an interview to the *Express*. (Eddowes was a dogged investigator who correctly identified John Christie as the real murderer in the crime for which Timothy Evans had been hung.) Eddowes had delivered a letter, he said, to Admiralty House, in which he informed them that Christine Keeler had told him that Ivanov asked her to get the date when nuclear warheads would be delivered to West Germany. And of course, she had been sleeping with Profumo at the time: by her own admission, Eddowes claimed, 'one used to go out one door while the other came in the other door'. He was exposing this in the press, he reported, since the intelligence services seemed to be doing nothing.

Keeler denied it; although Peter Wright, who interviewed her and later wrote about it in *Spycatcher*, said that her casual use of the phrase 'nuclear payload' certainly made him wonder.

In the second week of June, Stephen Ward was arrested and charged with living in whole or in part on the immoral earnings of Christine Keeler and Mandy Rice-Davies, in 1961 and 1962. He appeared at Great Marlborough Street Magistrates' Court on 17 June, was refused bail and remanded to Brixton. He was the son, reported the papers in astonishment, of a deceased Canon of Rochester Cathedral.

This story would run and run, right through June and July, and into August. The *Sunday Pictorial* kicked off by printing a copy of the 1961 letter from Profumo: 'Darling, in great haste and because I can get no reply from your phone ...' it began, and went on to apologise for unavoidable absence: '... until some time in September. Blast it. Please take great care of yourself and don't run away. Love, J.'

On 21 June, Macmillan instigated an enquiry, or – as he put it himself later – 'made the formal announcement about Lord Denning's appointment to an important but distasteful task, which he accepted out of pure patriotism. This led to at least some check in the flood of accusation and rumour.'

However, it didn't look like that to the great British public, who were being drip-fed great gobbets of revelation every few days. All sorts of people were brought into the affair. The Minister of Labour, John Hare, had lent Profumo the Mini, which he used to drive Keeler out to Richmond and other places on little jaunts. (The ministerial limo would not have done at all.) Prince Philip's name was linked to Profumo's in a banner headline, front page of the *Mirror* on 24 June: 'Rumour is utterly unfounded' was emboldened and underlined under a story that began 'The foulest rumour'. Before sharing the non-news that Ward had painted Prince Philip, Princess Marina and Princess Alexandra, and

– in big caps – 'APART FROM THESE PRIVATE SITTINGS THERE WERE NO FURTHER CONTACTS BETWEEN DR WARD AND THE MEMBERS OF THE ROYAL FAMILY CONCERNED'.

But could we be sure of anything anymore? 'Doctor' Ward was free on bail by the 4 July and arranging an exhibition of his portraits, which he hoped would pay for his defence. His Old Bailey trial was delayed while some witnesses talked to Lord Denning, but it positively rollicked along once it began. He was soon being accused of having arranged abortions. Every day a new floosie minced into the witness box; every day the papers printed pictures. Lord Astor apparently paid the rent on the Orme Court flat that Keeler and Mandy Rice-Davies shared, where Astor slept with Rice-Davies. In cross-examination, the prosecution dismissed this: Lord Astor said he'd never met her. 'Well he would, wouldn't he?' Rice-Davies responded tartly. There was a gale of laughter, a release of tension: everyone, awed a second before by the mere mention of an august personage, knew that she was right.

Douglas Fairbanks Junior turned up in statements, predictably, and so too did Peter Rachman, now dead, who had 'controlled my whole life' said Keeler. There were sub-heads about a two-way mirror and 'tying up and whipping', and about a girl who called herself 'The Chief Whip', since she did such good business at parties. Mandy Rice-Davies appeared to be wittier, smarter and more truthful than the rest. The idea that Ward was a pimp was ridiculous, she said. He hated even discussing rent, but would simply complain of poverty (usually after she'd had a man in her room) until some money was produced. But Christine Keeler was always borrowing money from him. Day after day, girls appeared; girls were 'being sought'; girls who had previously given lurid evidence withdrew it, saying that they had been subjected to pressure by the police.

Finally, it was time for the jury's deliberations, but Ward's lawyers did not hold out much hope. Ward was on bail, and staying with friends in Chelsea, when an ambulance was called. He had apparently taken an overdose of Nembutal. He remained in a coma for a week, his condition worsening rather than improving, and was found guilty in his absence of living off immoral earnings, but not of procuring. He died without ever regaining consciousness.

At his funeral on 9 August, 600 white roses were sent by a group of arty celebrities, including Joan Littlewood, Peter Blake, Alan Sillitoe and Angus Wilson, and dedicated to 'Stephen Ward. A victim of British hypocrisy.'

7

JULY – The Unthinkable

The Moors Murders

Ian Brady and Myra Hindley met at work in 1961. Both were cunning psychopaths. Brady, from Glasgow, had been neglected as a baby and more or less given away by this mother. He had been vicious all his life. As a child he dismembered and decapitated animals and as an adolescent, he had convictions for violence. Poorly educated, he taught himself book-keeping and was able to get a clerical job in his twenties.

Hindley was from Gorton, east of Manchester, a suburb of depressing back-to-backs dominated by a lowering nineteenth-century monastery; she was fascinated, as an adolescent, by Roman Catholicism. She had been farmed out to her grandmother after the birth of a younger sister. Her family lived in a near-uninhabitable slum and her father was violent. He rewarded her for fighting.

By 1961 she was a hatchet-faced, bottle-blonde typist of 19, and got herself a job at Millward's Merchandising in Gorton. (She seems never to have left the few miles east of Manchester in which she was brought up.) At Millward's she met Brady, who was 23 and thought a lot of himself. After circling around one another for many months, they began going out together. Dates at the cinema were followed by long discussions of the things that interested Brady: robbery, murder and Nazism. He gave her *Mein Kampf* to read. Brady's borrowed ideas, to her, were riveting. He glorified the individual's will to exercise total power over others; he made her think she knew more than other girls; she was exhilarated; they were an item, and he told her secrets.

In June 1963, they moved in together. He appears to have decided that the time for words was over, and the time for action had come. He wanted, he said, to commit the perfect murder.

Late on Friday, 12 July, a 16-year-old Gorton girl called Pauline Reade was reported missing. All the police knew was that her mother, Joan, was frantic. Pauline had gone out early that summer evening in a blue coat and white heels, intending to go to a dance at the Railway Club in Gorton. She had never arrived and nobody had seen her and there the case rested. The family were distraught, but life went on as usual for the people of Gorton.

As it happened, Pauline had been a friend of Myra Hindley's younger sister, and that night Hindley had pulled up in her van and offered her a lift. Pauline (according to Hindley) was in no particular hurry to get to the dance and willingly agreed to help Hindley with the errand she was on – a drive out to Saddleworth Moor to look for a glove. It was an expensive glove, and she'd lost it there. They got to the spot on the Moor, and almost at once a motorbike pulled up behind them. This was Brady, who had also come, Myra explained, to help look for the glove.

By the end of her life, Myra Hindley had given accounts of all five Moors Murders, the first being that of Pauline Reade. According to her, she was never once present at the killing; she was on every occasion in a room next door, running a bath, staring out of the window or otherwise distracted.

For this one, she stayed in the van while Brady went with Reade to look for her glove. After about half an hour he came back to fetch a spade. He told her where Reade was, and said she must go and sit with the girl. Myra did so and sat on the grass while Reade died. Her throat had been cut and it was obvious from the state of her clothing that Brady had interfered with her.

They buried her, and Hindley drove Brady back to Gorton in the van, with the motorbike in the back. On their way home they saw Joan and Paul Reade, Pauline's mother and brother, searching the streets.

Brady and Hindley had the weekend ahead of them, and went back to work on Monday. The penalty for murder, at the time, was execution by hanging. But there was no proof that a murder had happened; no body, no stranger in the area; the girl had just vanished.

Later that year, in the dark early evening of 23 November, Hindley and Brady were at the market in Ashton-under-Lyne. They invited a 12-year-old boy called John Kilbride to jump into Hindley's hired car for a lift home. They took a detour, on their way to his house, via Saddleworth Moor. Brady assaulted him sexually and then tried to cut his throat. When that failed he strangled him with a piece of string. The little body was buried on the moor.

On 2 December a four-line paragraph appeared in an inside column of the *Daily Express*. Over 2,200 people had searched until dusk at Ashton-under-Lyne, Lancashire, for 12-year-old John Kilbride, missing since visiting a local cinema nine days ago. The chief constable supervised the search, which was assisted by Civil Defence and a unit of Territorials.

Nothing was found. Hindley hired a car a couple of times that December, to drive out to Saddleworth Moor and check that the bodies had not been disturbed.

They murdered two more children the following year. Keith Bennett was a boy who disappeared without trace in June; his remains have never been found. Lesley Ann Downey was tortured and killed on Boxing Day, 1964. In 1965, when Brady lured a 17-year-old boy to their house and murdered him with an axe, there was a witness, and Brady and Hindley were arrested. They were charged with the axe murder, the Downey murder (of which they had tape recordings and photographs), and the murder of John Kilbride, whose name the police found at the house. Downey's and Kilbride's grave were found on the moor.

An interim law, designed to last for five years before review, came into force while Hindley and Brady were on remand; it meant that murder was no longer punishable by death. They were sentenced to life imprisonment, and abolition of the death penalty was made permanent in 1969.

The mystery of Pauline Reade's disappearance remained unsolved for twenty-two years. In 1985, after nineteen years in prison, both Brady and Hindley had learned to like publicity. They confessed to Pauline Reade's murder, and that of Keith Bennett. Two years after that, Reade's body was at last recovered from Saddleworth Moor. Keith Bennett's has never been found.

Hindley died in 2002 in prison, and Ian Brady is in an asylum for the criminally insane. Pauline Reade was buried in 1987 in Gorton Cemetery.

Kim Philby, the 'Third Man'

If the Profumo case could be dismissed as an embarrassment, the Philby Affair in July certainly could not.

The government line on Profumo was 'he had to resign because he *lied* to the House of Commons, not because we are prudish'. As long as they kept saying that, they diverted attention from Profumo's circumstantial link to Ivanov, the Russian attaché.

Philby was different. A weakened Macmillan government knew they were about to reveal at best complacency, and at worst criminal incompetence. International repercussions could be disastrous. Across the Atlantic, disillusion and derision were being confirmed by reports from former Russian spies that the British diplomatic and security services had been seriously leaky for years. If Harry ('Kim') Philby OBE, a double agent, had been actively spying for the USSR while leading the Brits by the nose, Britain's 'special relationship' would cool to freezing point.

British press interest had begun in earnest in January, at a time when Britain was struggling under a blanket of snow and smarting from de Gaulle's sneering dismissal of Britain's request to join the Common Market. A few weeks into the New Year, Kim Philby, a respected journalist, unexpectedly went missing from his home in sunny Beirut. Since 1956 he had been writing about the Middle East for the *Observer* and the *Economist*. He was well informed, well connected and very bright indeed; surely not the sort of person who had anything to hide?

Fleet Street was well aware that Philby was no mere journalist, but probably the 'Third Man'. Twelve years before, in 1951, two British diplomats called Burgess and Maclean had fled Britain for a new life in Russia. Donald Maclean, the more senior of the two, thus avoided, by about forty-eight hours, interrogation as a spy. Few in the security service had known this interrogation was to happen, but one of those who did – a mysterious and unidentified 'Third Man' working as a double agent – must have warned Maclean to get out fast; and Burgess was equally vulnerable. Treason was, in theory, a hangable offence.

Kim Philby was interrogated. Soon afterwards he resigned from the Foreign Office, and for the next five years he scraped a living as a freelance journalist.

In the House of Commons in 1955, Philby was verbally identified by Lieutenant Colonel Marcus Lipton, a wartime intelligence officer, as the 'Third Man'. Harold Macmillan, the then Foreign Secretary, personally denied it. So did Philby. Lipton apologised.

What certain individuals at the *Observer* also knew was that, within months of that exchange, Harry 'Kim' Philby had been recommended to them as a suitable Middle East correspondent. The *Observer* suggested to the *Economist* that they might employ him jointly, and he was hired. The initial recommendation had come through none other than the Foreign Office.

Fleet Street, and especially in 1963 *El Vino's*, was a parochial, gossipy place. The pack prised themselves away from the bar, got on aeroplanes and descended on Eleanor Philby, Kim's wife, who remained in Beirut with their children, and whose domestic bills were still being met by the *Observer*. In March, in response to repeated press queries, she claimed to have received a couple of cables, and some letters, from Kim explaining that he had been called away on an urgent assignment.

This came as news to the *Observer* and the *Economist*. Journalists investigated the most recent cable. It had been sent from Cairo, but Philby's signature was an obvious fake. The sender had given the address of a Cairo hotel, and its register did not contain the name of Philby or anyone who could have been him. An Egyptian government statement declared that he hadn't been in their country since 1962, and the Lebanese government had no record of his having left.

That was March. By May, a source in Cairo said that the Saudis were claiming he was on the Saudi-Yemeni border with the Yemeni royalist fighters.

Like Burgess and Maclean, Philby had spent several years in the 1940s in Washington as a diplomat; like them, he drank heavily; like Maclean, he was bisexual, while Burgess was homosexual; and like them, he had been educated at Trinity College, Cambridge in the 1930s. Nothing was proven, but there were a lot of coincidences.

Security leaks just kept on happening. In 1961, George Blake – who had been studying in Beirut – was exposed as a double agent. He was now serving a long sentence in Wormwood Scrubs. Since the mid-1950s, Peter Vassall, working in a quite lowly capacity for Naval Intelligence, had been blackmailed by the KGB, who had taken compromising photographs of gay sex. They used him in Moscow and London, and the thousands of documents he had revealed over seven or eight years had done immense damage. Only last October, he too had been jailed.

In June, *Isvestia* – then, with *Pravda,* an official mouthpiece of the USSR – repeated the story about Philby being with the Yemenis.

On 1 July, Macmillan had Lord Privy Seal Edward Heath make an important statement to the House of Commons. Kim Philby, he said, had been asked to resign from the diplomatic service in 1951 because of his past communist associations. He had admitted that he had been the 'Third Man' and a Soviet agent since 'before 1946'.

Uproar followed. Patrick Gordon Walker, the Shadow Foreign Secretary, demanded to know where, then, was Philby now? If he had been a communist since before 1946, surely he was unlikely to be working with the Imam of Yemen. And precisely when had he made this admission about being the 'Third Man'? A Conservative asked when, in the light of this and the Profumo Affair, they were going to have a minister for security? Macmillan was defenceless in the face of righteous anger. He claimed they were waiting to see what Lord Denning said.

Harold Wilson, Leader of the Opposition, was coruscating:

> In view of your appalling admissions that nobody told you anything, which suggests that the people under you didn't want to be told, and in view of the fact that even since the Denning enquiry was set up the Lord Privy Seal has been forced, by an American newspaper revelation, to make yet another statement, will you tell us now – assuming that you have enough judges to go round – whether you will appoint an enquiry into the Philby Affair?

'You really must learn to distinguish between invective and insolence,' Macmillan replied gamely. If every such revelation about traitors was greeted by fury, he continued, investigators would be put off. 'What has now happened is not a failure of the security services ... It is not a failure – it is a success!' Besides, he added, the Labour Party had been in power when Philby was active.

From 1945, that was true. But almost everyone present had served in the war. Many MPs were still known as colonel, commander and so on. They were well aware that lives were lost by treason.

It was now clear that when a significant Foreign Office official found Philby employment at the *Observer* in 1956, they already knew he had betrayed his country. It followed that they were still using him themselves, or, as George Brown put it: 'The Foreign Office is not normally an employment agency. Why did they do that? The only interest of the Foreign Office in this man being employed by somebody so that he could work in the Middle East could have been a Foreign Office interest in him working in the Middle East. What was that Foreign Office interest?' Edward Heath's response was, in so many words, 'Don't go there'.

The government had denied knowledge of Philby's past at least twice, when they obviously knew all about it, but he'd nonetheless duped them into thinking that, as a double agent, he had been well and truly turned to the British cause. Neil McDermott, a Conservative who had been in the Intelligence Corps during the war, demanded answers – and Macmillan fell back on a snobbish put-down. 'Tradition,' he chided, demanded that this sort of thing not be discussed in public.

Marcus Lipton MP had been vindicated eight years after his original question and Macmillan's negative response. Lipton now withdrew the apology to Philby that he had made in 1955.

The Americans seethed. The British press had a field day. Macmillan seems genuinely to have believed that Kim Philby was playing out a defection charade in order to dupe the Russians. This is what his memoirs imply; but nobody, apparently, knew where Kim Philby was.

'To betray you must first belong' is a saying attributed variously to George Blake and to Harold (Kim) Philby. Philby's sense of belonging had always been in doubt. He was his father's son in many ways, not least in serving more than one master at the same time.

Kim Philby had been born in the Punjab, British India in 1912. His father, Harry St John Philby, had been born in Ceylon, now Sri Lanka. (Ironically, Field Marshal Lord Montgomery, as plain Bernard Montgomery and a distant cousin of Kim's father, was best man at St John Philby's wedding in 1910.)

Kim Philby, a third-generation expat, went to prep school in India and then, like his father, to Westminster School and Trinity College, Cambridge.

Meanwhile, St John Philby, who spent his working life in India, Iraq and Arabia, became a British Intelligence officer and converted to Islam. By the 1930s, he was Ibn Saud's closest advisor in Saudi Arabia. In this capacity, he helped the Saudis negotiate a good deal from Standard Oil, encouraged the development of Aramco (the Arab American Oil Company) and generally cut out the Brits in favour of American interests. Nonetheless, he remained sufficiently well-connected in England to get Kim a job as *The Times*' correspondent for the Spanish Civil War. (*The Times* was then being edited by Geoffrey Dawson, who was pro-appeasement and forbade any mention in his paper of Hitler's anti-semitism.) Around this time, in the run-up to the Second World War, St John Philby managed to negotiate Germany's continuing oil supply from Saudi Arabia.

Politically, St John Philby was said in England to have 'gone native'; he was thought 'unreliable' on Jewish immigration to Palestine, joined the far-Right, pro-appeasement British People's Party on a brief pre-war sojourn in England, and failed to be elected as a British MP. He was in India when he was suddenly sent back to England and imprisoned in 1940.

Upon his release, he informed Valentine Vivian, the first head of MI6's counter-espionage unit, that it would be a good idea to employ Kim, who was then 28 and had all of his father's duplicitous charm. St John Philby and Valentine Vivian went back a long way; they were about the same age, and Vivian had been serving as head of the Punjab police when Kim was born there.

If Vivian's staff ever investigated Kim's background, they certainly found an interesting story. As a student, Kim had been a committed socialist, and by the time he graduated at the age of 21, the glamour of communism had seduced him. At the time it really was glamorous; Soviet Communism was still in the full flower of its youth, with terrific imagery, interesting films and art, and an almost religious fervour for progress, buoyed up by hope and good intentions. To someone shocked by the conditions of working people in industrial Britain, Soviet Communism must have looked like the solution to everything: the end of history.

Late in 1932, Kim Philby headed for Vienna armed with nothing more than a freshly acquired 2:1 in Economics, and a list of Comintern and other contacts supplied by his tutor at Cambridge, communist sympathiser Maurice Dobb.

Kim's task was to help with the evacuation of Jewish refugees. Once in Vienna, he fell in love with an Austrian girl, Litzi Friedmann, who had strong political convictions. Hitler came to power in May 1933. Kim Philby made the best possible use of his British passport in working as a courier between Vienna and Prague, delivering clothes and money to refugees from the Nazis.

In the summer of 1934, Philby and Litzi left for London as a newly married couple. Here Edith Tudor Hart (*née* Suschitzky), a Soviet agent, photographer, sister of the famous artist and friend of Litzi's, quickly recruited Philby to Soviet Intelligence. His first NKVD controller, Arnold Deutsch, asked him for a list of other likely recruits. Of the seven names Philby supplied, two stand out: Guy Burgess and Donald Maclean.

In London, Kim Philby – presumably with a diplomatic career in mind – enrolled at what is now the School of Slavonic and East European Studies. (This was again thanks to St John Philby, who was friendly with the director.) He also pursued a part-time career as a journalist, which meant developing close contacts within the German government and making frequent trips to Berlin. By the time he went to Spain in 1937, he and Litzi had arranged an amicable parting.

While sending *Times* reports from the pro-Franco side in the Spanish Civil War, and incidentally getting decorated by Franco, he was also providing information to the NKVD via Paris.

Back in London in 1939, he was so appalled by the Molotov-Ribbentrop Pact (under which Stalin and Hitler agreed to carve up Poland between them) that at the outbreak of war, his Soviet controller lost touch with him. Philby spent the next nine months as a journalist in England and France with the British Expeditionary Force. He returned to London within a day of the Dunkirk evacuation. He then worked for the War Office (where he ran into Burgess) until his unit was absorbed into the Special Operations Executive (SOE).

When, in 1940, he was sent to the spy school at Beaulieu to teach SOE operatives about clandestine propaganda, he reappeared on the radar of Soviet Intelligence. From then on, he supplied them with valuable information about Allied intentions. In 1941 he was back in London, working in counter-espionage for MI6 under Valentine Vivian, and running his own agents in the Iberian Peninsula and, later, in North Africa and Italy.

As Philby climbed ever higher in Whitehall, suspicion about him was voiced by at least one British officer and a CIA man. When a defector in Istanbul virtually identified him, Philby appears to have engineered the man's beating-up and rapid return to Moscow. But then there were suspicions on the Russian side too. Some concluded that all their agents in Britain, Philby included, were secretly working for the British.

Did the security services know that Philby was spying for the Russians during the war? It would seem so. In 1939, a former Soviet agent called Krivitsky testified before the predecessor of the House Un-American Activities Committee (HUAC). He was summoned to London in 1940 to speak to MI5. He told them that three Soviet agents had penetrated the Foreign Office, and one of them had been a journalist in Spain. Krivitsky was shot in a hotel room in Washington DC in 1941.

Either John Cairncross or Victor Rothschild, who served in MI5 and MI6 respectively in wartime, could have identified Philby from this description, but if they did, no action was taken.

When the war ended, Kim Philby and his new wife and family were posted to Istanbul; then to Washington, where as head of intelligence he worked closely with James Angleton, the CIA man who had been dubious about him in London. In Washington in 1950, Donald Maclean was identified as a possible Soviet informer. Philby tried to cover Maclean's tracks. Burgess arrived to work at the British Embassy: a disaster. Drunken, self-destructive and irresistible to the self-indulgent Philby, he caused scandal and was sent home. This disgrace quickly led to the final departure of Burgess and Maclean in 1951, and for Philby's resignation the same year.

When Philby was officially exonerated by Harold Macmillan in 1955, he gave a press conference. 'I have never been a communist,' he declared. As a lie, this ranks in history along with 'I did *not* have sex with *that woman.*'

So where was he now? The House of Commons had to wait a month for the humiliating truth. On 30 July 1963 came the official announcement from Moscow: Harold 'Kim' Philby had been granted political asylum and had become a citizen of the USSR.

London had seen the last of him; but the Philby shambles led to Harold Macmillan's eventual downfall. And one question remained unsatisfactorily answered: why had Philby suddenly fled from Beirut? Was there a fourth viper in the nest? The public were left wondering, but the government knew all along that Philby knew that his secret was out, and he'd been allowed to get away.

Dick White, the new head of MI6, had long been convinced that Philby was the 'Third Man', and Philby had confirmed this at a kind of old-pals-together confrontation with a British security officer by the end of 1962. He preferred not to sign a statement, though. The British officer, therefore, made a further appointment.

Between them, the three Cambridge Spies who had been exposed by 1963 – Burgess, Maclean and Philby (plus Sir Anthony Blunt who was not officially named as a spy until the following year) – had conveyed significantly useful information to the Soviet Union, of which the most damaging related to the Enigma codes during the early part of the war, and to atomic bomb progress from 1944 onwards.

Nonetheless, Macmillan's implied position, behind the scenes, was that the British planned Philby's defection scenario in the belief that he could continue to provide useful information from a new professional position in the Lubyanka. This seems unlikely, since by then Kim Philby was a desperate alcoholic. The Russians didn't trust him either, and kept him on ice, in what passed for decent accommodation in Moscow, for the rest of his days.

8

AUGUST – I Have a Dream

Civil Rights

America, land of the free, presented a sanitised view of itself to the world, but under the surface dissatisfaction was bubbling. In 1963, Rachel Carson published *The Silent Spring* and Betty Friedan *The Feminine Mystique*. Women, environmentalists and anti-war protestors were all increasingly frustrated with *de facto* government by what they saw as a patriarchal military-industrial complex. And that was just the white folks.

Throughout the summer of 1963 there were non-violent protests by blacks in the Southern states. The protestors maintained their dignity at all times and were careful not to break the law. Discrimination against African-Americans who tried to register to vote in states such as Alabama, Georgia and South Carolina included arrest and dismissal from employment. Public transport, schools, restaurants, banks and cinemas were segregated or barred blacks altogether. The Ku Klux Klan was active, and violent attacks by whites against blacks were common.

In February, President Kennedy had set out his plans for new legislation on Civil Rights. Black Americans would have the right to vote, discrimination would be outlawed and Federal action on all fronts would require desegregation. Legislation was necessary because without it, nothing had changed since emancipation 100 years before. Black children were growing up with the prospect of radically lower earnings, poorer health, inferior education and shorter lives than whites born at the same time.

Kennedy's moderate proposals were discussed by the judiciary and added to by interested state representatives and senators until the Civil Rights Bill was presented to Congress on 11 June. It would inevitably be delayed in the Senate by filibustering. The president suggested that both houses should just stay in session until the bill got through, but when the giant 'March for Jobs and Freedom' convened in Washington at the end of August, neither house had come to any decision.

The march was organised by five well-known pressure groups, of which the biggest was the NAACP (National Association for the Advancement of Colored People). There were a few militant Nation of Islam outliers, but they hardly signified; and names which later became emblematic of the 1960s – Stokeley Carmichael, Eldridge Cleaver and the Black Panthers – didn't figure at all. The march was, in conception and in execution, humble and dignified to the point of deference, and in that respect, it belonged to the 1950s.

A vast crowd of between 200,000–300,000 people, including many families with children, gathered at the Lincoln Memorial on Sunday 28 August, walked peacefully in their Sunday best to the Washington Monument, sang *John Brown's Body*, listened to spirituals sung by Mahalia Jackson and Marion Anderson, and responded to the speeches with applause and cheers. The whole event was overwhelmingly orderly, tidy and, on the face of it, about as revolutionary as a Sunday School picnic.

The Times of London was enchanted. It conveyed its impression that black Americans were 'just like us' only better behaved. 'At times the demonstration sounded remarkably like an inter-church assembly ... The assembly of rabbis could have shamed Tel Aviv and the Gandhi caps of the volunteer marshals served only to remind those with long memories how different this was from other demonstrations' their reporter announced in wonder.

1 Bridego Bridge, scene of The Great Train Robbery. (*Evening Standard*)

2 Tottenham Hotspur; by beating Athletico Madrid 5-1 they became the first British team to win a European trophy. (*Evening Standard*)

3 Clifton Junction, one of the 4,000 stations closed and abandoned as a result of the Beeching Axe. (Author's collection)

4 Great Train Robbers Bruce Reynolds and Jimmy White; both spent some years on the run until the law finally caught up with them. (*The Evening News & Star*)

5 The Duchess of Argyle, described by the Judge as 'a completely promiscuous woman whose sexual appetite could only be satisfied by a number of men'. (Author's collection)

6 Alcatraz Island Penitentiary, San Francisco Bay; closed by Attorney General Robert F. Kennedy in March 1963. (Author's collection)

7 'We Want Harold' … newly elected Labour Leader Harold Wilson kisses his wife after defeating rival George Brown. (Author's collection)

8 Christine Keeler, the 19-year-old model who brought down the government. (Author's collection)

9 Disgraced War Minister John Profumo returns home with his wife, actress Valarie Hobson, after his resignation. (Author's collection)

10 The 2,500-mile range A3 Polaris nuclear missile, described in Lockheed advertisements as 'a mighty force for freedom'. (Author's collection)

11 Jimmy Adamson, the FA's first choice for England manager. Like Alf Ramsey a league title winner; but would he have won the World Cup in 1966? (Author's collection)

12 The authorship of Ian Fleming's 007 novel *Thunderball* was to be the subject of a High Court case. (*Daily Express*)

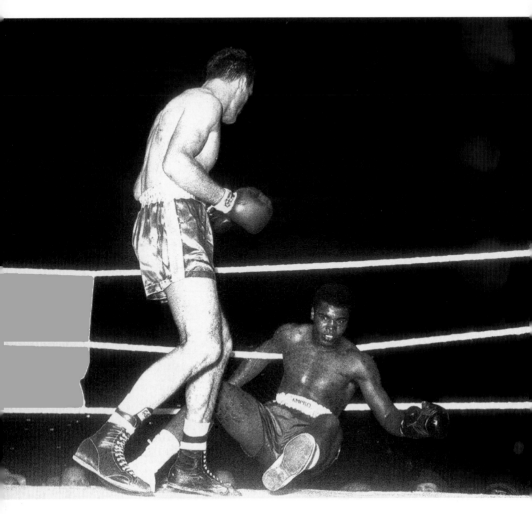

13 Muhammad Ali (then known as Cassius Clay) is knocked down for the first time in a professional fight by British champion Henry Cooper at Wembley Stadium. (*Evening Standard*)

14 Martin Luther King is arrested for 'trespassing' in a white's only diner. (Author's collection)

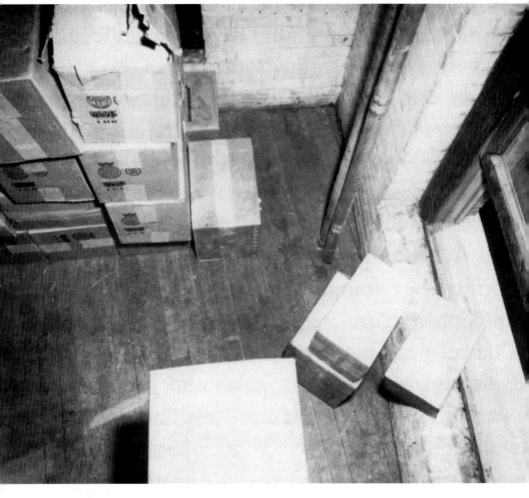

15 Warren Commission Exhibit 734, a bird's eye view of Lee Harvey Oswald's snipers nest on the sixth floor of the Texas School Book Depositary. (US National Archives)

16 A tireless campaigner; Labour Leader Hugh Gaitskell died in January due to over work and a mystery illness. (Author's collection)

17 Frozen in – the coldest winter in nearly 300 years freezes rivers, lakes and even coastal waters. (Author's collection)

18 Stoke City and Stanley Matthews win promotion back to the First Division. (Author's collection)

STAGE DOOR

Cummings

"Gentlemen, can't we persuade you to become Conservative candidates—after all, you've never had it so good!"

19 While this *Daily Express* cartoon featured Prime Minister Sir Alec Douglas Home, it was in fact Labour Leader Harold who courted The Beatles and later awarded them the MBE. (*Daily Express*)

20 The author celebrates his fourth birthday, 12 December 1963. (Author's collection)

Successive speakers stuck to ten clear demands. They wanted a minimum wage of $2 an hour and an end to discrimination in all walks of life. It didn't seem so much to ask. 'There is some reason for regarding the march as a gigantic safety valve designed to release the pressure and passion that, after a summer of intense but indecisive struggle, could have led to violence and bloodshed,' the man from *The Times* pointed out.

Yet the march worked. It gave added impetus to Kennedy, who met the leaders for an hour afterwards. But most of all, everyone left buoyed up with hope, dazzled by the optimism of Martin Luther King's 'I have a dream' speech.

On that day, the Reverend Martin Luther King was the most effective speaker of all. Already a legend for his leadership during the successful Montgomery Bus Boycott of 1955–56, he gave an address on behalf of the Southern Christian Leadership Conference. All the tropes of American Baptist preachers – rhetorical devices and Biblical language – were familiar to his audience, and they responded at once. 'No, no, we are not satisfied, and we will not be satisfied until justice rolls down like waters, and righteousness like a mighty stream,' he cried, quoting from the Book of Amos, and his words received a roar of approval. He took phrases from the Declaration of Independence and from Shakespeare. Most effectively, he used anaphora, repetition at the start of a sentence, to such rhythmic hypnotic effect that the crowd chanted their responses as they would in a Baptist church. Much of the speech was prepared, but the legendary 'I have a dream' part was partly inspired at the time by the elation and sincerity of the crowd:

Go back to Mississippi, go back to Alabama, go back to South Carolina, go back to Georgia, go back to Louisiana, go back to the slums and ghettos of our northern cities, knowing that somehow this situation can and will be changed. Let us not wallow in the valley of despair.

Let freedom ring!

Yeah Oh Lord Let Freedom Ring.

I say to you today, my friends, so even though we face the difficulties of today and tomorrow, I still have a dream. It is a dream deeply rooted in the American dream.

I have a dream that one day this nation will rise up and live out the true meaning of its creed: 'We hold these truths to be self-evident: that all men are created equal.'

I have a dream that one day on the red hills of Georgia the sons of former slaves and the sons of former slave owners will be able to sit down together at the table of brotherhood.

I have a dream that one day even the state of Mississippi, a state sweltering with the heat of injustice, sweltering with the heat of oppression, will be transformed into an oasis of freedom and justice.

I have a dream that my four little children will one day live in a nation where they will not be judged by the color of their skin but by the content of their character.

I have a dream today.

I have a dream that one day, down in Alabama, with its vicious racists, with its governor having his lips dripping with the words of interposition and nullification; one day right there in Alabama, little black boys and black girls will be able to join hands with little white boys and white girls as sisters and brothers.

I have a dream today.

I have a dream that one day every valley shall be exalted, every hill and mountain shall be made low, the rough places will be made plain, and the crooked places will be made straight, and the glory of the Lord shall be revealed, and all flesh shall see it together.

This is our hope …

This section of the seventeen-minute speech went out live and America was stunned. The following day's newspapers called King a great orator.

Not everyone was impressed. Alabama was notoriously racist with an anti-integrationist governor, George Wallace. The Klansmen of Alabama had no intention of allowing federal government to integrate their schools, and they prepared themselves for action.

The Great Train Robbery

When news broke, on Thursday 8 August, that 'over £2 million' in used notes had been stolen from a mail train, the British public were first astonished – indeed thrilled – and then amazed that it had never happened before. The train robbery, once the details were revealed, seemed such an open goal that you could practically hear half the population wondering greedily, 'Why didn't *I* think of that?'

In 1963, £2 million was a dizzying amount of money. Unimaginable wealth in the minds of most people was £75,000, which – according to posters on the sides of double-decker buses – you could win on Vernons Football Pools any Saturday. You could buy ten four-bedroomed freehold houses in London's leafy Holland Park for that. But over £2 million! It was unimaginable.

Cash was required for all but the largest transactions in 1963. British people had no plastic cards; in fact the vast majority had no bank accounts. Up and down the country, thousands of small traders carried their takings in cash to local bank branches. If they hadn't made it by 3.30 p.m. when the bank shut, they deposited their money in the Night Safe in the wall. The following day, bank staff counted and bagged the deposits.

These hundreds of thousands of banknotes were dispatched to a main railway station from which they were sent, every night, to the City of London for distribution to the relevant clearing banks. Since the days of the stagecoach, 'up' lines had been routes into London, so it was overnight 'up' trains from all over England that brought used cash to the City. For instance, parcels, letters and banknotes from towns around Glasgow, Aberdeen and Carlisle, and points south, would travel up the line to Euston. From a starting point at Glasgow, more coaches and mailbags would be coupled onto the train at a few big stations en route. Money and mail were separated, and sorted, on the train by scores of Post Office employees as they hurtled through the night. From Euston, the cash and the mail would be dispatched via mailrail (the General Post Office's (GPO) dedicated underground rail system) to King Edward Street Post Office and thence to the clearing banks.

After a Bank Holiday – such as Monday 5 August 1963 – there would be extra money aboard. The Glasgow mail was a diesel locomotive hauling twelve coaches. The first coach next to the engine was the parcels van, which had no communication with the coaches behind it. High Value Packets (HPV; bundles of money) were transported in the second coach, and this was connected by corridor to the ten mail-coaches behind.

The train left Glasgow at 6.50 p.m. on Wednesday 7 August, hauling parcels, the HPV coach and only the first three coaches; the other nine would join at Carstairs and Crewe. Extra staff came aboard or swapped shifts at other stations as far south as Tamworth. By 2.30 a.m. the train was speeding through a clear night on its run to Euston with seventy-seven GPO men aboard, a driver, fireman and guard.

At 2.53 a.m. it passed through Bletchley. Shortly after 3.00 a.m., the driver, Jack Mills, saw a warning signal ahead. A 'caution' lamp from a dwarf signal made him apply the brakes, and the red 'Stop' signal nearly a mile further on made him bring the train to a halt yards from the signal gantry at Sears Crossing.

The train was now less than 30 miles from Euston, stationary above flat fields on a raised embankment. The fireman, David Whitby, jumped down his seat beside the driver and headed over the rails to the trackside telephone, but quickly realised something was wrong. He shouted: 'The wires have been cut.'

Jack Mills later described what happened next:

[David] then walked back towards the cabin of the train. After David had gone back towards the coaches I saw two men come from the verge on the left hand side. I thought they were railway men. I could not see how they were dressed. It was too dark. I was looking at the controls of the engine and when I looked round I saw a masked man entering the cab on the same side as David Whitby got out; the left side. He had on a blue boiler suit and a balaclava helmet with just his eyes showing. I think the balaclava was green. He was carrying a large staff wrapped in white cloth. It was about 2 feet long. He was holding it ready to strike me, up in the air. I grappled with the man and almost forced him off the footplate. I was struck from behind. Someone came in from the other cab door. I do not know how many times I was struck. When I came to I was on my knees. The next I remember the cab was full of men. I was very frightened. One man wiped my forehead with a piece of rag. I could not see who they were; the blood was running in my eyes. They took me into the passage leading to the boiler room. They told me not to look round, not to look on the footplate. They told me to look that way, I would get some more if I did not.

This was the account that every news report emphasised. Without Jack Mills' testimony, the theft would have seemed – to a goggling British public – a victimless crime.

Even if you knew that the money was unguarded, this was a dauntingly difficult robbery to pull off. You had to stop a train, get inside it, overcome resistance, remove a bulky, heavy load of cash, and get away.

You must do this without being seen, heard or reported; you must leave no clues; you must go to ground afterwards without drawing attention to yourself or your money. In other words, your almost impossible task would be recruiting a large team of hard men capable of disciplined action, trustworthiness and discretion.

On the plus side, the money was used and unmarked, and if you arranged its successful concealment, you and your family would be secure for life.

No such successful heist could take place unless you got detailed, reliable and up-to-date information from somebody who worked (or had recently worked) inside the system. At some point in 1962, Brian Field, a young solicitor's managing clerk in a West End firm, discovered that he knew just such a person. He called his contact 'The Ulsterman'. The Ulsterman had been employed by the GPO and knew the Glasgow line well, he also knew how much money it carried. There could, he told Field, be between £2–6 million in cash on the 'up' train after a Bank Holiday; at any rate, well over a hundred mailbags.

Brian Field was a crook. He had underworld friends to whom he often passed on useful information about rich pickings, but there had been nothing remotely like this before. He approached Gordon Goody and Buster Edwards, career criminals. They met the Ulsterman and were excited by the prospect of untold wealth, but saw that they had a mountain of unanswered questions ahead and skills to supply.

They introduced two useful collaborators: Charlie Wilson, a formidable force in the underworld, and Bruce Reynolds, an intelligent leader. This mattered, since a platoon of criminals would be needed. But their generation had done National Service, so following orders was familiar.

Good organisation requires imagination and mastery of detail. Over the ensuing months, the leaders of the gang worked out where the train would be intercepted, how calls to the police would be prevented, how to take the loot away and where to take it to. Through preparatory robberies, they accumulated a war chest with which to finance the whole thing. They recruited men whose skills they would require, and to pre-empt any resentments, they made a deal. Everyone, from the inner circle to the least active participant, would get the same cut of the haul, whatever it was.

The robbery had to take place in the dark, in a lonely spot, somewhere on the long home stretch between Rugby and the Euston terminus. Sears

Crossing was isolated; you could stop a train at the signals and nobody would hear it or see it. Unfortunately, however, there was no road nearby and you would need, they worked out, at least three vehicles, including a truck, to take the mailbags away. The train must, therefore, be stopped at Sears Crossing, then the locomotive and first two coaches uncoupled and driven forward. The locomotive, parcels van and HPV coach would crawl along a couple of miles to Bridego Bridge, where the line ran over a road bridge, while members of the gang got the bags of cash ready for offloading.

They recruited a man who could tamper with the signals, and a former train driver. They also learnt from railway men how to uncouple the HPV coach from the ten behind it. They would then find somewhere deep in the country, a long way from the site of the robbery, where they could hole up undetected for a couple of weeks until the heat died down; supplies must be provided.

This was difficult. Twelve to fifteen men would have to get to the farmhouse under cover of darkness. To avoid later argument, all must be present when the bags were opened. The ringleaders drove around and scanned advertisements until finally Leatherslade Farm hove into view. This was the ideal, unoccupied, remote farmhouse, with running water and working sanitation, and it was for sale. Brian Field arranged for an offer to be made and a deposit was paid on the place. In the week they would stay there, people would inevitably see movement. The gang would put it about that the new owner had a team of decorators in the house.

When Jack Mills came to after being clubbed, he was still in the cab on his knees, surrounded by men arguing, and blood was running into his eyes. He was hustled down the passage to the engine room. The only light came from the driver's cab behind him, and he could see his colleague, the fireman, in the passage with a man in a balaclava. Somebody was trying to move the train, and failing. 'Well fetch the driver,' he heard. Next thing he knew, he was back in the driver's seat being told to move the train forward slowly and to keep his head down, not to look. 'And when we shout "Stop", *stop* or you'll get some more.' Mills had to release the vacuum brake – that was what had stopped the train from moving – and put the rear ejector on, which puzzled him; but he didn't know that most of the train was left behind.

He drove slowly on until somebody shouted 'STOP'. He still didn't know where he was when he was bundled out of the cab and down the passage to the engine room.

A big, angular, canvas-topped ex-army truck was tucked into the darkness at the bottom of the embankment below Bridego Bridge. Everything was going to a project plan, which was timed to the minute. Phone lines to the district had been cut shortly after midnight. Fifteen men (of the seventeen involved), in two Land Rovers and the army truck, had left Leatherslade Farm one and a half hours before, dressed as a platoon of squaddies in the command of a major – Bruce Reynolds had got himself the right uniform from somewhere. An army exercise would make the law back off, should any law be out and about at 3.00 a.m. Some of the robbers stayed with the vehicles when they got close to Sears Crossing, but others got out and headed across country to the railway line, wearing railway blue 'slop' jackets and trousers over their combat gear. They were variously tasked with re-jigging the signals, uncoupling the train, overcoming the driver and gaining entry to the HPV and the driver's cab. The one charged with driving it forward to the bridge had only worked on Southern Region trains before, and was unfamiliar with its vacuum-brake system, which is why he couldn't restart it. This was the first major hitch and a decision had to be made fast. The stand-in driver was shoved out of the way and Jack Mills shouted for and instructed to drive – they were off.

The five GPO men in the HPV coach knew that they'd come adrift from the rest of the train, but had no communicating door with the parcels van or driver ahead so they pulled the communication cord; it was all they could do. The train kept moving forward. Then it stopped. They could hear muffled voices ahead. Then – within feet of them, the loud smash of glass.

A window crashed inwards. A GPO assistant inspector yelled 'It's a raid!'

He and another postman raced to secure the rear corridor door, where already half a dozen robbers were trying to break in. They could hear shouting outside, and somebody yelling 'Get the guns!' and then robbers swarmed in through the doors, in through the windows, and the postmen were being clubbed to the ground. They obeyed the message: 'Lie still and you won't get hurt'. They were kept under guard on the floor at the front of the coach, quiet as mice, while they listened to mailbags being unloaded. The driver and fireman were shoved in to join them. Everyone present was told to keep still, or else.

Timing was crucial. The robbers needed the cover of darkness, so the money had to be unloaded fast. Sagging, heavy sacks were lobbed from man to man down the embankment and hurled into the army truck. Sweating, at 3.30 a.m. they had to go. Bruce Reynolds told them time was up. Six bags remained untouched in the train. They put the fear of God into the terrified staff, piled into the Land Rovers and the truck, and drove to Leatherslade Farm.

By 4.15 a.m. – no sooner, because it was half an hour before anyone reached the marooned HPV coach and because telephone wires had been cut – the police knew. Then Euston was informed. The story didn't arrive in time for the daily papers except under 'Stop Press', but it was on the BBC and in the evening papers (of which London had several at the time). The robbery was the hottest topic for years. Everyone knew where it had happened; that the driver had been badly injured; that it was a mail train; and that it was more than £2 million. But beyond that, there were only pictures of senior policemen at the robbery site, practically scratching their heads.

Five days later, however, came a breakthrough.

You're only as strong as your weakest point, and the gang's weakest point was post-event planning. They had been unprepared for the blanket coverage, for the significant rewards that were offered, and for everyone within a hundred miles of Bridego Bridge looking out for a big old truck, at least one Land Rover, and strangers offering to pay cash in unusually large amounts.

Nobody had stolen such a large fortune before and the robbers had had no idea that a storm of publicity would break. Nor had any of them much clue how to hide their cut of the loot. Scared by their own notoriety, instead of lying low before dispersing as planned, they fled from Leatherslade Farm after a few days, each man carrying suitcases and bags full of money.

The final clean-up of Leatherslade Farm was Brian Field's responsibility, but he failed to do it. When, five days after the robbery, the police were alerted to the three vehicles at Leatherslade Farm, items from a Monopoly board to a ketchup bottle were covered in fingerprints.

Soon afterwards, the first of the robbers was arrested, having paid three months' advance rent on a lock-up in ten-bob notes. And Brian Field was taken. On 16 August, a couple strolling in the woods near

Dorking found over £100,000 in a briefcase, a holdall and a camelskin bag. In the bag was a receipt. The receipt had Brian Field's name on it.

Once the wanted men were identified, most were quickly tracked down. They had underestimated the police. The man-hunt kept the case in the news for months, and when it eventually came to court, draconian sentences were passed. The Great Train Robbery did not end there, however; in the years that followed, more robbers were caught, while others escaped or gave themselves up, or, in the case of Ronnie Biggs (a minor player), escaped and made a career out of his notoriety. Several wrote books.

Four men were never caught. Just as big a mystery is what happened to the money. Comparatively little was recovered, and comparatively little remains to show for it in the families concerned.

With hindsight, the Great Train Robbery was an opportunity created by lax security, although there is no record of heads having rolled in GPO management.

Test Ban Treaty

After the Second World War, the American population were infantilised by censorship. The authorities did not want to 'disturb the tranquility' of the people. The most distressing still images, and what little film had been shot immediately after the bombings at Hiroshima and Nagasaki, were neither broadcast nor published.

Longer-term effects of the atomic bomb, such as repeated radiation sickness, cancer, sterility and birth defects, slowly did become known to those who chose to find out. Nonetheless, the arms race continued unabated, and by the mid-1950s both Russia and, to a larger extent, America, had stockpiled large quantities of death-dealing material. Both had nuclear bombs that were vastly more powerful than the ones dropped in 1945.

President John F. Kennedy knew that merely testing nuclear weapons in the remotest of locations could pollute the earth's atmosphere in ways nobody could control or even fully predict. Nuclear fallout (the popular term for radioactive dust resulting from explosions) did not degrade quickly. Nobody knew how long its ill-effects would remain potent, or precisely what happened to the human body when exposed to it for a long period of time. As to the nuclear waste produced by nuclear reactors, it was routinely buried in the ground in cardboard boxes, from which it leached into soil and water. In 1959 there were reports of radiation-contaminated wheat and milk in parts of North America.

In 1955 the UN had tried to initiate discussion concerning a nuclear test ban, but this had foundered on Soviet unwillingness to allow inspectors onto their territory. Even so, in 1960 during his presidential campaign, Kennedy had made a point of arguing for a worldwide ban on nuclear testing. He had another agenda besides immediate health concerns: a test ban would bring, he thought, an end to nuclear proliferation. Understanding of atom bomb technology would be restricted, as far as possible, to those few countries who already had the science, the raw materials and the money. On the whole this meant the USA and the USSR, who were already confronting one another in a Cold War. Should they ever deploy their atomic bombs, mutually assured destruction was inevitable.

There was a moratorium on testing between 1958 and 1961. But in 1962 the Cold War warmed up, as the USA and the USSR began to play chicken over Cuba.

In 1959 the Cuban dictator, Fulgenicio Battista, had been ousted by Fidel Castro, who was supported by the Russians. In 1961 Kennedy made an ill-advised decision to support anti-Castro Cuban exiles in an invasion. The idea was that they would wrest power back from the Communists; they failed and most were taken prisoner.

Kennedy and Khrushchev met. Khrushchev, conscious that he held the moral high ground, showed himself belligerently determined to seal off West Berlin from the rest of East Germany; or else, he threatened war. Kennedy was humiliated, which did his standing no good at home, and in the autumn the Soviets tested a weapon 4,000 times more powerful than the one that had wiped out Hiroshima.

Kennedy held his nerve and challenged the Russians 'not to an arms race, but to a peace race'. When that didn't work, America resumed atmospheric nuclear testing of its own in the spring of 1962.

That summer, Fidel Castro taunted the Americans and thanked the Soviet Union for its backing. There were rumours that the USSR had provided medium-range missiles to Cuba, which turned out to be true. Kennedy protested. Russian intercontinental ballistic missiles (ICMs) were then spotted there.

An American spy plane crashed on the island. The Russians protested, and piled on the weaponry pointing at the US mainland 90 miles away.

In late October, tension escalated to a nail-biting point. American forces were one step away from full alert. This time, Kennedy did not flinch, and suddenly there was a climb-down on both sides. The US would undertake not to invade Cuba, and to remove its missiles from Turkey (although this was initially a secret undertaking). In turn, the Russians undertook to remove its missiles from Cuba. The world breathed a sigh of relief.

Kennedy and Khrushchev had scared the living daylights out of one another. It was as if Khrushchev, at least, had come to a belated realisation of what Kennedy had known all along – that it was within their power to destroy tens of millions of people.

Fortunately, both leaders were sane. Both saw the idiocy of destroying the world in order to save it from the other. They began, at last, to communicate. In the summer of 1963, after what in diplomatic terms were brief negotiations in Moscow, a draft agreement was reached by key ministers of the USSR, the USA and the UK. On 26 July, the *Daily Mirror*'s front-page headline read:

They agree – at last!
Britain, America and Russia finally agreed last night on a treaty banning the nuclear tests which shower the world with deadly radio-active dust. This great agreement was initialled in Moscow about 5.15pm after ten days of talks – breaking a 5-year deadlock.

The interim agreement was initialled by Lord Hailsham, Andrei Gromyko and Averell Harriman. The *Mirror* piece continued:

... The treaty prohibits all nuclear tests in the atmosphere, in outer space and underwater. It does not cover underground tests, because the Russians refuse to accept international inspection.

The *Mirror* was a Labour paper. The Labour Party, many prominent British intellectuals, thousands of students, Quakers and some Anglicans backed the Campaign for Nuclear Disarmament (CND), which was then at the height of its influence and popularity. The annual CND march from Aldermaston to Trafalgar Square at Easter was attended in huge numbers (by a protest song-chanting rabble that looked to Middle England like duffle-coated beatniks, but still, there was a canon of the Church of England in there, so they had to be tolerated). The agreement was a long way off CND's ultimate aim of British unilateral disarmament, but a positive step forward nonetheless.

On 6 August, with the official signatures due to be set down, it was the *Daily Express*'s turn to be euphoric: 'An ending of the Cold War between Russia and the West seems to be in the making here in Moscow tonight.'

It was a *limited* test ban treaty, but still it was progress. Dean Rusk, Lord Home and Gromyko did sign it the following day; and on 8 August, twenty-one more nations signed in Moscow, twenty-four in London and thirty-one in Washington.

According to the *Express* correspondent in Washington, the Americans saw this treaty as a signal that Khrushchev had 'turned his back on Chinese militancy'. It was true that the Soviet Union allied to China would have made a formidable enemy. But Khrushchev, who knew perfectly well what the results of enforced collectivisation had done to the Soviet Union under Stalin, had had reservations about Mao's brutal policies for a long time. China was a place of brutality and famine, and in 1963 it remained effectively isolated even from the Soviet Union.

9

SEPTEMBER – Thunderball

The Denning Report

When, on 4 June, Profumo had revealed that he had lied about his affair with Christine Keeler, Macmillan suffered a perfect storm of emotions. In January, the spy Kim Philby had been allowed to disappear; an intelligence officer had got him to admit his guilt, then let him go. What could be better calculated to make the security services look out of control and the prime minister too weak to call them to account? In March, Macmillan knew that the Profumo scandal had once again shown how out of touch he was – the last to hear rumours that had apparently been buzzing around the House since January. He had taken Profumo at his word. Henry Brooke had supported Hollis's assertion that MI5 hadn't needed to get involved, with sexual peccadilloes not coming within the service's remit. But after the Stephen Ward revelations, Macmillan began to think he should have challenged both Profumo and Hollis. In addition, a Cabinet minister had been mentioned in the disgraceful Argyll divorce. Sandys denied it, but was nobody to be trusted? Everyone Macmillan knew (not just the man in the Argyll case) seemed to be wearing a mask. It all combined to make him look as if he wasn't on top of his job. And these scandals made him feel particularly squeamish. 'I do not remember,' he confided to his diary 'ever having been under such sense of personal strain. Even Suez was "clean" – about war and politics. This was all "dirt"...'

The more he thought about it, the more obvious it became that MI5 had been asleep on the job – or worse. He therefore summoned Dick White, whom he trusted, and asked him if he was being set up by Soviet intelligence. (Sir Dick White had preceded Sir Roger Hollis as head of MI5 and was now head of MI6.) White did not believe that Macmillan needed to worry on that score, but he needed to set his mind at rest. On 17 June, a joint MI5-MI6 working party was instructed 'to look into the possibility that the Russian Intelligence Service had a hand in staging the Profumo Affair in order to discredit Her Majesty's government'.

As to further revelations that were emerging out of the Lucky Gordon trial and the Mandy Rice-Davies case in June, it was all more than he could stand. Macmillan, therefore, turned to Lord Denning.

Lord Denning, master of the rolls and a law unto himself, who once said 'We have strayed too far from the path of our fathers. Let us return to it. It is the only thing that can save us...' would conduct an enquiry 'out of pure patriotism'. He was 64 years old, had his prejudices, weaknesses and areas of ignorance, loved his work, and would live to be 100.

The day after Macmillan called in Lord Denning, Duncan Sandys, son-in-law to Sir Winston Churchill, minister for commonwealth relations and MP for Streatham, felt moved to confess in Cabinet that it had been he who had volunteered himself for medical examination in the Argyll divorce case; not because he was the man in the pictures, but because of rumours going about. One more damned thing.

In the cliché of our time, not theirs, we would say that Denning hit the ground running. The question to which he sought an answer, in 55,000 words, by mid-September, was: had national security been imperilled by the conduct of any minister? What Macmillan was guaranteed was a good read, as Denning famously knew how to tell a good story.

He had a list of names, which quickly grew: 160 people were to be interviewed. As he later recalled, 'I saw ministers of the Crown, the security service, rumour-mongers and prostitutes. They all came in by back doors and along corridors secretly so that the newspapers should not spot them. Some of the evidence I heard was so disgusting – even to my sophisticated mind – that I sent the lady shorthand writers out, and no note of it was taken.' The self-proclaimed 'sophisticated' mind of Lord Denning was boggling off the scale. Before July was out, the Ward trial had been postponed for a week so that he could see Ward and some of the witnesses first. ('He's the nicest judge I know,' simpered Mandy Rice-Davies when she emerged.)

He also asked for papers relating to the Argyll divorce. Macmillan had at last, after Sandys revealed that rumours had mentioned his name, developed a capacity for scepticism. He had asked Lord Denning to establish whether the 'Headless Man' might in fact be Sandys.

Five men were called into the Treasury to speak to Denning about the Argyll case, among them Duncan Sandys and Douglas Fairbanks Junior. All five were requested to sign the Visitors' Book as they came in from Whitehall. Then they were interviewed. Since Duncan Sandys had already offered to be medically examined, and the only possible means of identification was comparison of his pubic hair with that in the masturbation picture, testimony from a man in Harley Street quickly ruled him out. But Denning's cunning plan went further. The 'Headless Man' photographs all had writing on the back. By comparing the handwriting with the Visitor's Book, he decided the man in all the photographs had been Douglas Fairbanks Junior. This conclusion was redacted, but he was at least able to reassure Macmillan on the Duncan Sandys question (falsely, as it turned out; before she died, the Duchess of Argyll drily remarked that the only Polaroid camera in this country when that photograph was taken had belonged to the Ministry of Defence. Duncan Sandys had been Minister of Defence from 1957 to 1959. He was the headless man in the fellatio picture, Douglas Fairbanks the headless man in the masturbation one.)

More witnesses came, including Edgecombe and Gordon. Denning was quite dewy-eyed about Christine Keeler, who, poor defenceless young thing, had become 'enmeshed in a net of wickedness' before she was 21. Special Branch had got hold of a thirteen-hour tape recording of Christine Keeler talking, and someone in authority took a more jaundiced view of her than Denning did, since on 4 September, two weeks before the report was finished, Keeler, another working girl called Paula Marshall and their housekeeper, were arrested. Keeler was charged with perjury and conspiring to pervert the course of justice.

By then Denning had retired to his country house to complete the report. The 55,000 words were typed and delivered to the prime minister and Harold Wilson on Monday 16 and Tuesday 17 September respectively. They would discuss it, and agree on any revisions, and it would go to press in time for publication on 26 September.

Discussion of Denning at the Conservative Party Conference in October was banned.

On 26 September at 12.30 a.m., there were apparently 120 people queuing on Kingsway, outside HMSO, for the report that would become a best-seller.

That day, the *Express*'s banner headline shrieked:

It's Dynamite!

In a 55,000 word report written with the skill, bite and suspense of the best detective novel, Lord Denning comes out today with a two-way verdict on Mr Macmillan and his government over the Profumo case.

That was the exciting part. It was all downhill after that, for the report was a non-story almost on a par with the Prince Philip portrait one.

No minister had been 'immoral'. All rumours about ministers of state, even one about a minister and little boys, were dismissed out of hand. None of these men were named. The security services were completely exonerated. Scotland Yard was chastised because it had not been well co-ordinated. And one gentle remonstration: surely the five Parliamentary colleagues who had interrogated Profumo in March should have asked to see the letter to Keeler, rather than just accepting that there was nothing in it?

Denning concluded: 'This was an unprecedented situation for which the machinery of government did not cater. It was, in the view of the security service, not a case of security risk, but of moral misbehaviour by a minister. And we have no machinery to deal with it.'

So, that was that. Hollis had been right all along. As to Sir Dick White's investigation into a possible sabotage of the security service, by the time that it reported in the negative, Macmillan had resigned through ill health. He was not, however, the last to question lapses in efficiency during Hollis' tenure, and allegations and rebuttals persist to this day.

The Deep South

The federal government under Kennedy was determined to enforce desegregation. There was an anti-liberal, aggressive culture among whites in the Southern states, and many were embittered by what they saw as Washington's tyrannical interference in their affairs.

Their champion in Alabama was Governor George Wallace. Wallace was a determined segregationist, although by nature he was not the most vicious white supremacist in the state. Post-war, sitting as a judge, he had had a reputation as a 'liberal'. In a 1958 gubernatorial Democratic primary, his opponent John Patterson got Ku Klux Klan support, while Wallace was backed by the National Association for the Advancement of Colored People (NAACP). He lost, and told a friend: 'I was outniggered by John Patterson. And I'll tell you here and now, I will never be outniggered again.' He became a hardliner, and in January 1963 succeeded in becoming governor. In his inaugural speech he declared:

I draw the line in the dust and toss the gauntlet before the feet of tyranny, and I say segregation now, segregation tomorrow, segregation forever.

In Huntsville, Alabama, schoolchildren began the new semester early in September. Four elementary schools were to be desegregated despite Wallace's protests. Sonnie Wellington Hereford IV, whose own father had fought hard to get into medical school and qualify as a doctor, later wrote:

When I arrived for my first day of school as a first-grader in Huntsville, Alabama, in 1963, my entrance was blocked by the governor. In fact, George Wallace closed all the Huntsville schools that day rather than have a black boy enroll at one.

Whites continued to seethe with outraged frustration nonetheless. There was a street in Birmingham, Alabama, called Dynamite Hill because so many racist bombings had occurred there, and on the night of Wednesday 4 September, the house of a black lawyer was blown up. The local black population poured onto the streets and they were angry. Governor Wallace ordered 200 state troopers to intervene, a man was shot dead, and there was a full-scale riot. After that, no appeals from black leaders could hold the mob. 'Sustained firing over the heads of the crowd has introduced an uglier and more dangerous phase,' reported the London *Times*.

All the children turning up for school were sent home. Wallace petitioned the federal court for a 'stay' of its desegregation order. He failed. Sonnie Hereford wrote:

> The governor relented a few days later, but only after my family had made another visit to federal court in Birmingham, allowing me – on September 9, 1963 – to be the first black child to attend a previously all-white primary or secondary public school in the State of Alabama.

One of the elementary schools to which black children were able to return that Monday 9 September was boycotted by two-thirds of the other pupils; and at another school, the black children and their teachers were the only ones who turned up.

Birmingham, the state's biggest city, was thriving thanks in part to a large pool of non-unionised black labour. The city boasted that it had many, many churches, which it would have, as the number was at least doubled by segregation. Its 16th Street Baptist Church had recently been used as a centre for the desegregation campaign led by Martin Luther King and others. On the morning of Sunday 16 September, a bomb exploded in the church after Sunday School, about five minutes before people began to trickle in for the religious service. Four girls aged from 11 to 14 were killed.

This was reportedly Birmingham's twenty-first racial bombing in eight years. The 16th Street Baptist Church was the seventh black church to be attacked, and three bombs had been thrown at the homes of black clergymen. Its pastor said:

> We have been waiting for it, knowing it would come, wondering when ... I have received half a dozen bomb threats since last April. We searched the church several times. We called off night-time meetings because we felt it would be just too dangerous, even if only to pray ...

Events would follow a pattern that was already familiar: black people would pour onto the streets to protest against some hostile act of violence – this one, a bomb big enough to damage buildings across the street – and as on this occasion, their leaders would calm them down. Sometimes, also as on this occasion, State troopers would arrive in their hundreds on the orders of Wallace because of his 'fear of reprisals'. Nobody was arrested. The police said yes, they accepted that men had been seen in a car, but their identity was uncertain; they could have been white, but then, they could have been Mexicans or negroes.

That evening in Birmingham, a black boy of 16 was shot dead by police who said he had been throwing stones, and a black boy of 13 lost his life in a drive-by shooting by one of two white boys on a scooter. A total 1,400 national guardsmen, state troopers and police amassed on the streets.

The FBI sent investigators. Kennedy was outraged. The NAACP demanded effective federal intervention and Roy Wilkins, executive secretary of the NAACP, sent an exasperated telegram to Kennedy:

If we are not to have more than picayune and piecemeal aid against this type of bestiality, please tell us now so that we can marshal such resources as we possess and employ such methods as our desperation may indicate in the defence of the lives of our people.

The president sent an assistant attorney general to speak to Wallace. (An assistant attorney general is third in rank below the attorney general.) On 20 September he also sent a 'committee' of two peacemakers, whose task was to get black and white communities to talk to each other. One of them was a former secretary of the US army, and the other was a former football coach at West Point.

Sympathy for the victims of the church bombing had an effect. In 1964, most of Kennedy's Civil Rights Bill finally passed into law. For many years, Birmingham, Alabama, like many other Southern cities, remained, on the whole, as fiercely dismissive of civil rights for blacks as it had ever been, but shame was expressed for the church bombing nonetheless, and local schools did start to accept black as well as white pupils.

Four Ku Klux Klan members had planted the dynamite, with a time-delay mechanism. One was identified within weeks, arrested and charged with murder. He was found not guilty; he got off with a $100 fine and six months' imprisonment for having possessed the dynamite. The case was re-opened in the late 1970s, when the same man was brought back to court, re-tried and jailed. He died in prison in 1985. In 2000, three others were also named as perpetrators; two were still alive, and were arrested, tried and jailed.

Fylingdales

September saw the opening of Britain's first ballistic missile early warning station at Fylingdales in Yorkshire. It was one of three, ultimately controlled by the US air force; the other two were in Greenland and Alaska.

The thinking behind it was both defensive, and co-operative. The co-operative part had begun, like so much of Britain's political direction, during the Second World War with the Atlantic Charter of 1941. In the face of a crazed dictator in Germany, a totalitarian ally in the Soviet Union and an aggressive Japan, Roosevelt and Churchill drew up and signed a charter of general principles for a better post-war world.

Implicit in this was co-operation through intelligence sharing, an aspect formalised in 1946 by the UK-USA agreement. In other words, if Russia decided to attack America and the British found out first, they'd flash the news to the Americans (and Australia, New Zealand and Canada would sign the same agreement). By 1946, with the Iron Curtain descending over Eastern Europe, the nuclear arms race moving fast, and the start of the Cold War, the enemy was clearly the Soviet Union.

Defensive motivation was stepped up dramatically in 1957 when the USSR launched Sputnik, the first satellite. If the Russians could put a satellite into space and bring it back to a target, they could launch nuclear missiles from the Soviet Union which would cross the Arctic and hit the United States.

Intelligence demanded a warning of any such attack, and Fylingdales – built by RCA – was third in a string of radar stations that would provide it. To the British public, they were supposed to provide a 'four-minute warning'. Until then, British and American defence against nuclear missile strike had consisted of valuable radio tracking operated from Jodrell Bank in Cheshire, plus (for use in case of attack) secret underground bunkers, command centres, plans to commandeer broadcast media and so on. Civil Defence taught the public that if early warning sirens went off, then they had to go indoors, switch the radio on and shelter under the dining room table.

Seen across the Yorkshire moors, Fylingdales looked like three vast golf balls neatly lined up by a giant from outer space. Each of the golf balls was a geodesic dome containing a mechanically steered radar scanner measuring 40m across. Uniquely, Fylingdales provided 360 degree coverage to a distance of 3,000 miles.

It worked around-the-clock for all but thirteen hours until 1991. With a true early warning system permitting retaliation and, therefore, deterrence, America's Mutually Assured Destruction nuclear stance brought peace (and an arms race) for as long as the Cold War lasted.

The Robbins Report

Access to higher education in 1963 was rare and highly valued. The state education system worked on the principle of elimination. At the age of 11, the eleven-plus exam effectively excluded 75 per cent of children from later expectations of education beyond the age of 15. Children of better-off families were educated privately, along a scale varying from small prep schools to the great public schools like Eton, which retained a reputation for excellence.

The 25 per cent who succeeded at the eleven plus would go to grammar schools, with some of them 'grant-assisted'. Of the other 75 per cent high-achieving secondary modern pupils could theoretically get promoted to a grammar school, but very few did. Many of their pupils went on to apprenticeships in industry, or simply gained skills in a lifetime of work. (Since all the 75 per cent were comfortingly supposed to be 'good with their hands', some towns had secondary technical schools as well.) Until the 1970s and '80s, it was common to find under-qualified British managers of the post-war generation in industry and commerce, and a MBA (master's degree in business) was not expected.

In the grammar schools, Latin and often ancient Greek were taught, but not business studies or economics; the subjects were pretty much those that had been usual in 1900, with more science and mathematics. About half of a grammar school's annual input would go on at 18 to take the Advanced ('A', and even higher scholarship 'S' level) exams. About three-quarters of those who passed their A levels would go straight into office jobs or the service industries, or colleges where they would get diplomas in subjects like teaching or engineering; girls were expected to go into nursing, teaching or on to secretarial colleges or art schools.

The very highest achievers, most of whom were boys, would attend Oxford, Cambridge or London University, often after passing further entrance exams. Long-established universities like Nottingham, Bristol and Edinburgh were just a gnat's whisker lower in the pecking order; and then there were the so-called red-bricks like Birmingham and

Southampton. East Anglia (due to open in October) and Sussex were daringly new.

But only 4 per cent of all British 18-year-olds, including those who were privately educated, would go to university at all. This constant narrowing down of the field had inbuilt class and gender bias in many forms. It shaped the profile of the workforce in which almost all professional lawyers, architects and doctors, for instance, were male and middle-class.

The Robbins Report ('Report of the Committee on Higher Education'), which appeared earlier in the year but was accepted by the Government on 24 October, sought to change all this. Lord Robbins was an economist who had been Chair of Economics at the London School of Economic since 1929, and he and his committee had spent two years on the report. He failed to understand, he later wrote, how 'a government which is pledged to abolish artificial hierarchy and invidious distinction in the schools, should be actively engaged in preventing the elimination of artificial hierarchies and invidious distinctions in higher education.' The result of this 'active engagement', in his view, was visible in the vastly different professional outcomes of those who went university and got a degree, and those who went to technical colleges, art schools, teacher training colleges and so on. Britain's human resources, in other words, was being squandered in a way that no economist would approve. Universities 'should be available to all who were qualified for them by ability and attainment'.

The report recommended that universities should take more students and that CATs (Colleges of Advanced Technology) should have university status. In fact, the initial rise in numbers was to be quite gradual – from 197,000 students starting their first degree in 1967, to 217,000 starting in 1973. So, only 20,000, or about 10 per cent more students a decade went to university, but this continued to rise thereafter.

This apparently gentle increase would, he hoped, ensure that standards did not slip or universities become crammers. He insisted that research should not suffer, and that they should continue to promote 'the general powers of the mind, so as to produce not mere specialists but rather cultivated men and women'. On that point, he urged massive investment in the arts at the same time. As for postgraduate education, he explained the principle beautifully: 'In the graduate school there are no ultimate authorities, no orthodoxies to which the pupil must subscribe.'

His fast lane to a better educated workforce would be the further education colleges. Many (other than the CATs) would have to raise their game, so that degree-level courses would be available at polytechnics, teacher training colleges and so on. In due course, this did take place. While accepting that some universities would always remain more eminent than others, Lord Robbins sought to improve access to the best education for all.

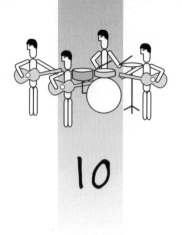

10

OCTOBER – It's My Party

Sir Alec Douglas Home

Macmillan, with great deep folds over his outer eyes, pouches beneath them, and a heavy moustache, managed to give an impression of anxiety. Lord Home, who succeeded him, had skin tight across a skull-like face and a weak chin, which made him look timid. Both prime ministers were easy targets for cartoonists of the day, despite the fact that Macmillan could be humorous and Home assertive.

Harold Macmillan had been 'SuperMac' to them once. The 1950s caricature of the prime minister in Superman costume had been ironic, but it came to be seen as a cheerful image of Macmillan single-handedly rescuing Britain from its wartime doldrums; releasing it from its colonial burden when he noticed 'the wind of change blowing across Africa'; and promoting home markets (boosted by consumer goods bought on the never-never) by persuading the electorate that 'you've never had it so good'.

Macmillan had been a favourite of Churchill and epitomised unflappable, upper-class *sang-froid*. But battered by Vassall, Philby, Profumo, and the satire boom reflecting public disillusion with complacency at the top of British public life, he seemed, by the autumn of 1963, undermined and weary. He was not at all well; he had prostate trouble.

The Conservative Party was getting worried about his capacity to lead them into a General Election the next year. Lord Home, who was Foreign Secretary and an old friend, suggested that Macmillan might want to confirm to the Party that he did, in fact, want to carry on. Macmillan was confident; certainly he did. He'd give them a pep talk at the Party Conference in October and everything would be fine.

It was not, however, because on the night of 7/8 October he was taken to hospital with severe prostate trouble. He was forced to withdraw. On 9 October Sir Gerald Nabarro, a Tory MP never known to mince his words, told a Conservative meeting in Bolton, 'Britain cannot be governed and led by a sick septuagenarian'.

Macmillan, genuinely ill, resigned the following day. Within hours of the news breaking, Quintin Hogg (Lord Hailsham) declared an interest in the job. This did not go down at all well with some Tories, who felt Hogg was bumptious and over-pleased with his own cleverness, which is how the public often saw him as well. In contrast Rab Butler was an obvious successor to Macmillan. He had been passed over for the job before, but his inconsistent performance and pre-war history, tainted as it was by appeasement, still divided the party. He didn't give a good conference speech, although his supporters, who were many, stood by him.

The old guard, the inner circle of influential Tories, were dismayed by Hailsham and turned to Lord Home. He had made it clear he wouldn't stand; he liked his job and liked being in the House of Lords. He was, after all, the latest earl in an ancient line and he'd have to renounce his title and win a seat in Parliament at a bye-election – 'a convulsion in my life for which I was ill prepared,' as he later wrote mildly. Nor would he welcome the strains of office, especially the need to appear economically competent, which he wasn't.

Chancellor Reginald Maudling was, in Home's words, 'the best equipped in economics' and was a moderniser, keen to get business booming; his most recent budget had been expansionist and he was riding a wave of popularity.

On the whole, though, Macmillan and the Tory grandees would decide. Hailsham's vulgarity had offended them; Rab Butler would divide the party; and Maudling was too junior and maybe too volatile. Lord Home, with whom the public was not familiar, it would have to be, and so it was. He conceded that he would stand, and he won.

Irritatingly, his name was pronounced Hume. He would become Sir Alec Douglas Home instead of the thirteenth earl. Harold Wilson, Leader of the Opposition, taunted him about the title. Home's quick riposte was addressed to 'the thirteenth Mr Wilson'.

To the public, Alec Douglas Home was an unknown quantity, and so he remained; he never did have the common touch and, despite his best efforts, the Conservatives would lose the 1964 General Election, albeit by a whisker.

Beatlemania

General awareness of The Beatles, beyond people under 18, had risen steadily between February and October, and then had soared. On 7 December, at 6.00 p.m., all four made up the *Juke Box Jury* team, and at 8.00 p.m. the same evening they had their own show on the BBC. Both programmes were shot at the Empire Theatre, Liverpool, during The Beatles National Fan Club Convention.

In February, an article about Northern pop hadn't even featured their name in the headline. By December, if a sub-editor put 'BEATLES' into block caps he attracted readers. They were at Nos 1, 2, 7, 11 and 19 in the hit parade.

They also attained that Holy Grail of rock 'n' roll publicists: adverse comment in the House of Commons. Henry Price, Tory MP for West Lewisham, was seriously worried about the effect of Beatles music on the nation's youth: 'We must offer teenagers something they will like better ... it has a hypnotic effect on them. Their eyes become glazed, their hands wobble loosely and their legs wobble just as loosely at the knees. This is known as "being sent".'

October had marked the tipping point. On the 13th they had topped the bill of a weekly TV institution, *Sunday Night at the London Palladium*. It was an hour-long live show in front of an audience, broadcast at peak time. The show that night broke all precedent by having the star act on first, for a few seconds only. Compere Bruce

Forsyth then stuck his long chin round the curtain: 'If you want to see them again,' he confided, 'they'll be back in forty-two minutes.' They came on again forty-two minutes later, did their act, leapt aboard the revolving stage at the end – and were gone.

Fifteen million people had watched them at home. People only had two channels to choose from, but still, 15 million was high even for this popular show.

Next morning, every mass-circulation British newspaper carried a front-page picture and story of rioting Beatles fans outside the London Palladium. 'Police fought to hold back 1,000 squealing teenagers,' the *Daily Mirror* gasped, 'as The Beatles made their getaway after their Palladium TV show.' Both the *Daily Mail* and *Daily Express* carried an obviously set-up, tall, narrow portrait of the four Beatles, one grinning face above the other, 'peeping' out in supposed dread of a 'mob', this time said to number 500. 'A Police motorcade stood by,' squeaked the *Mirror*, 'as the four pop idols dashed for their car. Then the fans went wild, breaking through a cordon of more than sixty policemen' (the *Express* said twenty). The fans were girls who 'flung themselves' at The Beatles, and 'boys dressed in high-necked tight-fitting Beatles type clothes … With engines racing, the cavalcade roared down Argyll Street and turned into Oxford Circus, heading for a celebration party at the Grosvenor House Hotel.'

The stories weren't about how well or how badly the group had played their songs, but simply about the chaos they had caused.

This official outbreak of Beatlemania in Britain had certain puzzling aspects. In every case, the published photograph of the thousand squealing teenagers was cropped so close that only three or four could be seen. The *Daily Mail* alone published a wide-angle shot – Paul McCartney and Neil Aspinall emerging from the Palladium, watched by one policeman and two girls.

'There were no riots,' Dezo Hoffman says. 'I was there. Eight girls we saw – even less than eight. Later on, the road managers were sent out to find The Beatles a girl each, and there were none.'

'From that day on,' says Tony Barrow, their press officer, 'everything changed. My job was never the same again. From spending six months ringing up newspapers and getting "No", I now had every national reporter and feature writer chasing me.'

From then on, his job entailed simply selecting, along with Brian and other press officers who were later used, journalists who were *allowed* to interview The Beatles. On 22 October, the man from the *Mirror* was permitted an audience with Epstein himself, in a Park Lane hotel room, and made a full-page feature of it.

Epstein's presentation of The Beatles to this reporter reflected something that had been going on for a long time in British pop: what you might call the 'Archbishop tendency'. The liberal middle-aged were always trying to understand 'youngsters' and Adam Faith, a good pop singer in his day and a better businessman later, had famously been interviewed by some senior cleric on the Sunday night television. This sort of thing was supposed to reconcile the old folk to the 'Youth of Today', who might appear scary but were really nice lads underneath, with souls.

There was no way The Beatles could lose street cred by telling some reporter how nice and unthreatening they were; down 'n' dirty London bands like the Rolling Stones were coming up in the outside lane. So it was Epstein, the record store owner, who stood in as the civilised face of popular music. 'I definitely think The Beatles are an art form' said this 'elegant and cultivated young man' who had, we were impressed to learn, spent eighteen months at RADA. He had seen The Beatles at the Cavern.

'Quite frankly,' he said, flicking a speck of dust from his silk socks, 'I thought they looked a mess.' They had jeans and long hair but were 'very attractive'. Whether or not the rest of the interview was verbatim is hard to say, but it included a lot of quotes from Epstein speaking in the third person 'One's artistes ...' and using words like 'frightfully'. Did he really sound so posh? He explained how he'd got George Martin to hear them in 1962 and talked about Cilla Black and his 25 per cent He seemed reassuringly amiable, capable and honest.

There was a drip-feed of news after that, and photographs, which definitely looked genuine, of 7,000 Beatles fans trying to buy tickets for a concert in Newcastle. That story was supported by a picture of a girl in the crowd who had fainted. On 31 October, the *Mirror* reported that Alan Owen would be writing the screenplay of a film for them; that Walter Shensen would produce it, for United Artists, and it would cost £200,000 to make; that shooting would start 'on their return from Paris in February'.

True or not, what did it matter? By then, half the bedrooms of schoolgirls in England were papered with Beatles posters and cuttings.

11

NOVEMBER – Conspiracy of One

The James Bond Court Case

James Bond, the tall, dark, enigmatic British spy, was devastatingly handsome; the hearthrob of 1963 as played by Sean Connery. As Bond his screen persona was captivating, his adventures daring beyond belief, his sophistication breathtaking, his powers of seduction envied by every man old enough to have a working mojo. Hollywood producers Cubby Broccoli and Harry Saltzman were on to a winner that would run and run.

James Bond had been the hero of two movies since 1962, and both had played to packed houses worldwide. They were fast-moving fantasies, with characters exaggerated to cartoon proportions, horrifying reversals of fortune, locations in paradise, and James Bond a man of rat cunning and imperturbable cool. In *Dr No*, a spellbound audience learned that a martini must be 'shaken not stirred' to be worth drinking, and that Ursula Andress arising from the waves in a bikini was a jaw-dropping sight. *From Russia with Love*, released in October, introduced SMERSH, the Soviet Intelligence agency with its evil and deeply unattractive agent Rosa Klebb, whose pointed shoes concealed flick-knives. It was terrific stuff, and all the better for never quite taking itself seriously.

Audiences were enormous. There wasn't a lot to do after dark in most British towns, and nowhere to go on a date except the cinema. Boys were fascinated by this older man who could make girls come across – such girls being rarer than hen's teeth in their own lives – and girls saw that there might be some fun in it, too. It was escapism, but also a battle between good and evil in which good was just bad enough to be interesting.

With the success of the Bond films came renewed interest in the books that had inspired them; and of course in their wealthy, glamorous author, Ian Fleming, with his home on a Caribbean island and his shady past in intelligence work.

In November, with *From Russia with Love* packing them in at the cinemas, the news broke. Ian Fleming, the real-life James Bond, was about to appear in the High Court, accused of plagiarism. It was hard to believe, for Ian Fleming was convincingly knowledgeable about Bond's world. He had been born into the eponymous merchant banking family, although, despite a lively mind and extraordinary opportunities, he had been too idle to make much of his life until the age of 31. Only with the outbreak of war in 1939 did he find his direction. His organisational skills, social circle and imagination made him a valuable asset to Naval Intelligence. Among other important successes, he came up with the idea for Operation Mincemeat (in which a corpse, set adrift and later retrieved, was used to plant false information in Nazi minds).

After the war he became foreign manager of the Kemsley Newspapers group, which owned the *Sunday Times*. He had a reputation as a faithless roué, and had a winter home, Goldeneye, in Jamaica, where he spent three months of every year.

In 1952 he returned to London having written *Casino Royale*, the first of twelve James Bond books. Jonathan Cape published it and it was reprinted several times. It was followed by others, and Columbia optioned (though did not make) a film of *Casino Royale*.

His books were popularly successful, but towards the end of the 1950s Fleming's work was getting biting reviews from critics. His marriage was shaky, his health poor, and his literary nerve failed. He resigned from his job and did hack work for Kuwait Oil, which was rejected as too contentious.

It was, professionally, a low point, but by then he had met Kevin McClory. An Irishman, McClory was much younger than Fleming and a skilful film scriptwriter. Fleming had never been able to master writing for film and he was running out of plots, so he agreed to collaborate on a James Bond film based on an idea of McClory's. Much of the on-screen action would take place underwater and Bond would confront his most terrifying opponent yet. McClory and Fleming worked on it from 1959 to 1960 when Jack Whittingham, a British writer, was brought in to help McClory.

What McClory and Whittingham did not know was that, when Fleming disappeared that year for his usual over-winter at Goldeneye, he would write a new James Bond book, *Thunderball*, with pretty much the plot and characters that all three had devised. He would complete it, send it to his agent and have it accepted for publication by Jonathan Cape. It was published in 1961, copyright Ian Fleming.

McClory and Whittingham were stunned; he hadn't said a word to them. They sued at once for breach of copyright, confidentiality and contract, false representation of authorship and 'slander of title', which meant essentially that Fleming had passed off their intellectual property as his. Before the case was heard, Whittingham assigned his rights in his now-completed screenplay to Kevin McClory, and agreed to fight alongside McClory as a witness.

Producers Cubby Broccoli and Harry Saltzman, with the backing of United Artists, sailed blithely over all this. They found a third writer, American Richard Maibaum, to construct a script based on the McClory-Whittingham script and the Fleming book. They didn't bother to obtain any rights; they just asked Maibaum to get on with it. When in 1961 Sean Connery was first approached about playing Bond, this was the script he saw.

In November, journalists and photographers crowded around the Royal Courts of Justice. Fleming was urbane. Certainly, he told the court, he had based *Thunderball* on a script being prepared by McClory and Whittingham, but it was McClory who'd asked him to do so. McClory had rung him up in 1959 and asked him to write the book of the as-yet-unmade film, in order to help sell it to producers.

This, McClory said, was patently untrue. *Thunderball* was almost completely derived from Jack Whittingham's script which he, McClory, owned. It was plain from reading the book alongside the script that Fleming had made clumsy attempts to disguise Whittingham's plot, location and characters, and that none of these, as written by Fleming, could possibly have proved acceptable in a book that was supposed to promote, or in some way reflect, an eventual film. Much of Fleming's book was either un-visual or un-filmable, and simply altering the script had left holes in the plot, which had been filled in with irrelevant scenes.

Witnesses were heard in the Chancery Court for more than a week, with the author and his entourage decamping daily for lunch at the George, across the road.

Perhaps Fleming's lawyers recognised that the court seemed minded to agree with McClory. Not only was his a convincing case, but if Fleming's claim that he'd merely been doing McClory a favour by writing the book of the film was true, how could Fleming also claim that McClory had no right to the story? Or perhaps – as his friends said – Fleming was simply too ill to carry on. Also the vehemence and effectiveness, and financial resilience, of McClory may have surprised him. Anyhow, nine days into the trial, proceedings were suddenly adjourned.

It was Friday afternoon, 30 November. Lawyers negotiated throughout the weekend and a figure was agreed: Fleming would pay £50,000, a huge sum, in damages. The world heard nothing until Monday, when it was announced that a settlement had been reached. The following day, by order of the court, Fleming assigned and sold the copyright to the novel *Thunderball*, and 'all the copyright in the film scripts and the exclusive right to re-produce any part of the novel in films'. All future editions of the book would have to include the words 'Based on a screen treatment developed by Kevin McClory, Jack Whittingham and Ian Fleming' (in that order).

Fleming was very ill indeed by this time. He had heart trouble and nine months later, aged only 56, he died. Kevin McClory first issued a licence for the use of *Thunderball* material in a film in 1965; it went to Eon, the Broccoli/Saltzman production company, and was for one film only. All rights would revert to McClory after ten years. In 1983 McClory produced a new adaptation of the *Thunderball* plot: *Never Say Never Again*.

Coup and Assassination in Vietnam

French colonial forces had been driven out of 'Indochina' (broadly speaking the South East Asian peninsula) in the early 1950s, and since the Geneva Accords of 1954, Vietnam was divided into North Vietnam and South Vietnam.

North Vietnam was a Communist state, agrarian, authoritarian and prone to famine. As far as its leaders were concerned, South Vietnam was an allegedly democratic state that was supported by America: a colony in disguise. North Vietnam encouraged the Viet Cong, a small but highly motivated guerrilla force, which operated in the forests and mountains of the South, to distract, provoke, sabotage and ultimately destroy the régime.

The US, which in principle supported democracy against communism, saw South Vietnam as a buffer against Chinese expansion into South East Asia. The Chinese had already pushed east into North Korea, and were employed in building roads out of Tibet down to South East Asia. They were amassing troops on the Himalayan border with India, and they supported agitation in Indonesia to remove Sukarno. The US government had since the war perceived a Chinese Communist threat from that part of the world and was concerned that Russia and China should not unite.

America rewarded the leaders of South Vietnam for taking a strong line against the Communist Republic in the North. Power in the South was held by two brothers from the Catholic Ngo family. Ngo Dinh Nhu was head of the secret police and Ngo Dinh Diem was the president. Diem had taken the senior position after defrauding Nhu of an election win in 1955, and held onto it. Both had been born into the country's royalist elite. Diem had never married or made much of a name for himself until the 1950s.

Although Ngo Dinh Nhu was in charge of the security service, it was Nhu's wife Madame Nhu, a Catholic convert from a wealthy Buddhist family, who got most of the publicity in the foreign press. She was believed to be the autocratic influence that directed Diem's thinking.

By 1963, the South Vietnamese army was engaged in an increasingly bloody struggle against the Viet Cong. It was supported by a steadily rising number of well-trained, well-equipped US troops: about 16,000 at the time.

Vietnam was traditionally Buddhist and there were monasteries in every town. The Ngo brothers made sure that Buddhist families were disadvantaged at every level. Key jobs usually went to Catholics and Buddhists were routinely imprisoned, tortured and accused of spreading Soviet propaganda. The West was horrified in June 1963 by a vivid expression of despair: a Buddhist monk doused himself in petrol and set himself alight in a street in Saigon. Even the aggressively anti-communist American media had no doubt that this public self-immolation was a protest against the cruelty of Diem and Nhu. In August, the Americans were appalled by particularly nasty attacks on monasteries in Saigon and Hué. Buddhist monks had been organising non-violent protests against their persecution for weeks, and they had mass support. Nhu and his cronies commanded heavily armed soldiers to raid the monasteries with grenades and machine guns to wreck the Buddhist protest. Hundreds of monks and nuns died or were injured.

The foreign press had been forewarned; all this had been timed to take place in the absence of effective American presence – the US Ambassador had returned home and his replacement, Henry Cabot Lodge, had yet to arrive. Madame Nhu said the defeat of the Buddhists was 'the happiest day of her life' and Ngo Dinh Diem proclaimed a victory; the monks, he said, had been amassing arsenals of weapons in their monasteries.

Madame Nhu, in Saigon, was interviewed by Donald Wise of the *Daily Mirror* more than once. She was portrayed as Cruella de Ville, a role in which she seemed to revel:

This fabulous 5ft 2in mother of four … has never looked happier … A flick of her fan has more punch to it than a clout with a rifle butt. 'Power is delightful. Absolute power is absolutely delightful' she told me. 'If I had an atom bomb I would use it on the Communists.'

The way things were going, she might just get one. But after those raids on the monasteries her family disowned her, the *New York Times* printed the pro-Buddhist view of their columnist David Halberstam alongside the official South Vietnamese Government version, and Kennedy and his advisors – unconvinced by the Ngos for a while now – changed American policy. The Ngos were out of control, irretrievably. On 24 August, Lodge was quietly advised to think of their overthrow as a possibility that America would not oppose. In September, the Americans threatened to withdraw funds. Early in October, an American senator and a general on a fact-finding US mission arrived to talk to Diem about the possibility that US assistance might be cut back. He didn't seem to get the point.

Significantly, they also had a word with General Minh, known as Big Minh. Minh, with a loyal following and a mouthful of gold teeth, made it clear that a coup, and an assassination, might work. The CIA did not express vehement opposition.

Donald Wise put a face to the story in the *Mirror*. He saw Madame Nhu again and wrote this time about:

> ... her hate-filled black eyes ...vain, puritanical, imperious and wily ... She has seen to it that 6,000 crack troops have been pulled back into towns to fight their own people. Meanwhile 16,000 American 'advisors' continue fighting Red Guerillas at a cost of £500,000 daily ...

How, asked Wise rhetorically, could the Americans expect to defeat communism with her in charge?

Was Madame Nhu really a power behind the throne? The beleaguered Buddhists certainly thought so; she was widely hated. However, when (on 1 November) fighter bombers attacked the presidential palace, fourteen generals led by Minh staged a CIA-supported coup, and American warships were said to be racing towards the South China Sea – Madame Nhu and her children were safely in Los Angeles. Her husband and brother-in-law, at the height of the fighting in Saigon's streets, were both shot dead in the back of an army truck the following day.

It was time to leave the USA: 'I cannot stay in a country which has stabbed my country in the back!' Madame Nhu shrieked to the newspapers, releasing a carefully chosen set of pictures of herself as a tender mother. She spent her exile in Paris and Rome, and lived to be 87.

The poisonous Ngos had gone, but South Vietnam's government was never stable after the coup. The North Vietnamese felt they had won a propaganda victory, for after this there could be no possible doubt about the fact that the South was a puppet state.

The Assassination of President Kennedy

November 1963 saw a moment in time that was probably more examined, discussed, argued and written about than any other in the twentieth century, including the dropping of the atom bombs at Hiroshima and Nagasaki.

The undisputed facts were these: President Kennedy and his wife Jacqueline were wildly glamorous, independently wealthy, clever, eastern-seaboard liberals, visiting Texas. On Friday 22 November, at approximately 12.30 p.m., they were in Dallas. They were in a motorcade passing through Dealey Plaza; crowds had come to see them. President and Mrs Kennedy were waving from the back of an open limousine. Gunfire was heard. The president was fatally shot.

This, and the resultant panic and speeding up of the motorcade, were recorded by an amateur film-maker in a twenty-six-second sequence forever afterwards known as 'the Zapruder film'. The cars sped off to the Parkland Memorial Hospital where, in the emergency room, the president was pronounced dead from a gunshot wound to the head.

Governor Connally of Texas had been travelling in the same limousine, in a seat in front of the Kennedys, with his wife; he was also shot, and severely wounded, but recovered. Vice President Lyndon B. Johnson was two cars behind and was not shot at.

Security men immediately raced up the 'grassy knoll' that rose alongside Elm Street next to the motorcade, but caught nobody. One witness was certain that shots had come from the Texas Book Depository on Elm Street. Lee Harvey Oswald, who should have been at work there, was reported missing. A high-powered rifle was found discarded on the sixth floor. An hour and ten minutes after the shooting, Lee Harvey Oswald was challenged in a street 3 miles away by a police officer. He shot the officer dead. Lee Harvey Oswald was subsequently arrested and found to be armed with a pistol.

Still wearing her pink Chanel suit stained with her husband's blood and brains, Jacquie Kennedy accompanied her husband's body back to Washington in Air Force One. 'I want them to see what they have done,' she said.

Oswald insisted to police that he had shot nobody, that this was a case of mistaken identity, and that he was being blamed because he had at one time lived in the Soviet Union. Two days after the assassination, handcuffed and surrounded by police and television cameras broadcasting live, Oswald was being moved from the police station to Dallas County Jail when Jack Ruby, a local nightclub owner, emerged from the crowd and shot him dead at point-blank range.

On examination, the rifle found at the Book Depository proved to be the one that had fired the shots that killed Kennedy and injured the governor; it was marked with prints from Oswald and fibres from his shirt.

The assassination had a backstory and an aftermath. The immediately evident background was political. The Kennedy/Johnson Democrat ticket had won by a very small margin in Texas. In Dallas, a notoriously Right-wing Republican stronghold, Adlai Stevenson – a UN Ambassador and high-profile Democrat – had been deliberately struck by an anti-UN protestor only a month previously. Nonetheless, the visit, which was already in the diary, was necessary; there was a presidential election next year.

The day's schedule had been as follows: the Kennedys would fly in from Fort Worth in Air Force One, the jet that went with the job; and they would spend a few hours in Dallas and have lunch, before flying out to Austin. Kennedy's purpose in Texas generally was to raise funds, boost the morale of local Democrats (they were divided, which wouldn't do his campaign any good) and, in particular, to court popularity with the man on the street. He was intending, when he spoke in Dallas, to make a clear statement on domestic policy. That night at a dinner in Austin, he would have stated the direction of his foreign policy. Both these speeches would have been curtain-raisers to the president's campaign for re-election in 1964.

In view of the Stevenson incident, security was tight; but not so tight that the motorcade route was not made public a couple of days beforehand, with the stated aim of creating a welcome; or so tight that a team of local homicide detectives were tasked with following the car, which would have been expected – they were not.

Oswald was arrested rapidly and almost, it seemed, by sheer good luck. Before any security failures or details about him were made public, theories were springing up like weeds after rain. An assassination in Dallas, a hard-line city, instantly made many people suspect a Right-wing plot. Cuban exiles and many anti-communist American Republicans were pretty angry with Kennedy. The Cuban Missile Crisis, in which Kennedy and Khrushchev had negotiated a way out of nuclear war, had happened only last year, and, as a result, America would not be backing an invasion of Cuba any time soon.

The revelation that Oswald had lived in the Soviet Union for nearly three years put a dent in this idea before suspicion morphed into a conspiracy theory (that Right-wingers had framed Oswald for a murder that they in fact had committed). Republicans counter-claimed that the killing was obviously a Soviet plot to destabilise America.

So, within days, the aftermath – numerous conflicting conspiracy theories, which would lead to an entire book-of-the-assassination genre in publishing – had begun. The nation mourned. Tributes flooded in from all over the world. Vice-President Lyndon B. Johnson found himself thrust into office.

The state funeral was held at Arlington Cemetery, and hundreds of millions watched it on television. The flag-draped coffin was drawn by white horses. Jacquie Kennedy wore a black mantilla and walked behind the caisson with Edward and Robert, Jack Kennedy's brothers. During the Requiem Mass in the cathedral beforehand, she clutched the hands of her little girl and boy in their velvet-collared English overcoats. All remained dignified. As theatre, the funeral would have melted a heart of stone.

The apparent assassin was dead, but still questions swirled unchecked. How many shots had been fired? And from where? Who were the bystanders, caught on film and in photographs, who had never been identified? Was the rifle a plant? Had Oswald been the gunman? Had the gunman, whoever he was, acted alone? If not, who fired the shots? Who ordered the shootings? Who was Jack Ruby? Had he been acting on orders to shoot Oswald? What exactly were the post-mortem and ballistics findings? Who had allowed the Dallas police record of Oswald's questioning to be so inadequately undertaken? Who was behind it all – the CIA, the FBI, anti-Castro factions, leaders of the military-industrial complex, the Mafia? Jack Ruby knew Mafia people. Had Oswald been set up?

President Johnson was sworn in, and got busy organising the war in Vietnam. He set up a commission of enquiry under Judge Warren to supply answers to the questions about Kennedy. J. Edgar Hoover ordered the FBI to prepare its own investigation of what must have happened; this came out less than three weeks later and was in some obvious respects inadequate.

The Warren Commission reported ten months later, and in September 1964. Both this and the FBI enquiry concluded that Oswald, acting alone, shot Kennedy, and that Ruby had been acting alone when he shot Oswald. There was no stoppering the bottle though. The first conspiracy book had been published six months before the Warren Commission and sold well. As more film and photographs turned up, and as files leaked out in the decades to come, there were more investigations, official and unofficial, and more books often focusing on the roles of the CIA and the FBI. In 1976, the House Select Commission on Assassinations (which looked at the deaths of Martin Luther King and Robert Kennedy, as well as Jack Kennedy) concluded that there had indeed been a conspiracy, but it was impossible to say who was involved; certain nations and organisations could be ruled out, but that was not to say that a band of rogue individuals could not have plotted the murder.

The last book on the subject has not yet been written. Investigating the assassination has become an industry akin to that surrounding the identity of Jack the Ripper, and the part of Dallas where it happened has become the Dealey Plaza Historic District. As Robert Dallek wrote in his critically acclaimed *John F. Kennedy: An Unfinished Life* (2003):

> To this day, a substantial majority in America assumes that an aggrieved group rather than just Oswald was behind Kennedy's killing … To accept that an act of random violence by an obscure malcontent could bring down a president of the United States is to acknowledge a chaotic, disorderly world that frightens most Americans.

Doctor Who

When Sidney Newman, a well-regarded Canadian television producer, came to Britain in 1958 to work, the third of the BBC's hugely successful six-part *Quatermass* serials was about to begin. *The Quatermass Experiment* had been broadcast live in 1953 (before competition from independent television was allowed) and *Quatermass II* in 1955. This last serial, *Quatermass and the Pit*, with sound effects by the BBC's new Radiophonic Workshop, would be the most successful of all; 11 million viewers watched the sixth episode. The serial was terrifying, gripping and wildly imaginative, an irresistible alliance of esoteric myth and sorcery (Dennis Wheatley's occult thrillers were best-sellers then) with science fiction set in real places, and real situations, familiar to millions.

Newman had arrived in a country which had only two grainy, 405-line monochrome channels, operating for roughly ten hours per day, in fierce competition; the BBC had to justify the licence fee paid by everyone with a working TV set, and the independents had to raise money from advertisers. The TV you saw depended on where you lived. Granada, for instance, in the north-west, would, from 1961, gain a huge following for its soap *Coronation Street*, which was successfully sold to other independents, but many programmes were never exported elsewhere. Newman had an excellent track record of producing bankable, fast-moving drama, some of which had already been bought for British television. He was contracted to work for ABC until the end of 1962.

He therefore had plenty of time in Britain to form an opinion, and on the whole he was unimpressed by the state of BBC television drama, which had not kept pace with the new, grittier writers who were producing work for theatre and screen; its TV plays were stagey, drawing-room 'Anyone-for-tennis?' stuff of a kind to which he was strongly averse.

So, when, in January 1963, after an extended head-hunt, he became Head of Drama at the BBC, he came in like a whirlwind.

First he broke up the Script Department, which had become rather precious about the allegedly rare skill required to write for television, as opposed to the theatre or the cinema. He split the Drama Department into three: Plays, Series and Serials, each of which would be led by a single individual eager to commission something original, popular and relevant. Plays would always be single, one-off events (opera was included under Plays). Series, broadly speaking, were 'plays' in that they contained stories with a beginning, middle and end, but 'serials' in that they followed a core line-up of characters or a crucible location throughout several episodes. Serials were usually weekly productions, ending on a dramatic crisis that required resolution in the next or subsequent episodes. They were not necessarily soap operas, although some, like *Compact,* set in the editorial office of a magazine, went out fifty-two weeks a year.

Newman then instigated the system that had inspired harder-hitting TV drama in America and Canada. The producer's role changed. Until now, a BBC drama producer had been expected to produce, direct and liaise with the writer on the script. This might work in a village hall, but he foresaw more ambitious productions that would stretch the medium, and the resources of one controlling mind. Entirely different skills and talents were required at each stage of production.

From now on, each production would have three key creative managers assigned to it. The script editor, director and producer would work together on the overall vision: the concept, who would write it, and how the broadcast outcome should be presented. The script editor would approve the script and liaise with the director. The director would choose actors, direct the shoot and (where film was involved, although much drama still went out live) work with an editor in post-production. The producer oversaw the project and its budget, acted as go-between and public face of the programme, and generally made sure that the final concept, from titles to credits, appeared on screen at the scheduled time.

ITV had been going for eight years by the time Sidney Newman became BBC TV Head of Drama. The BBC had better sports coverage than any of the independents, especially on Saturday afternoons. Newman wanted to hang firmly onto that audience before the BBC's hit show *Juke Box Jury* began. God forbid they should switch over; if they did that, he'd lost them for the evening. The BBC football results signed off the Saturday sport, and were usually followed by a dramatised version of a children's classic story. The hour between 5.00 p.m. and 6.00 p.m. was 'Children's Hour' and was sacrosanct, but the current content could be moved to Sunday if he could only find something that worked for 1) sports fans 2) children 3) teenagers waiting for *Juke Box Jury*. He wrote later:

... I was intent upon it containing basic factual information that could be described as educational – or, at least, mind-opening for them. So my first thought was of a time-space machine (thanks to H.G. Wells) in which contemporary characters (one of whom I wanted to be a 12–13-year-old) would be able to travel forward and backward in time, and inward and outward in space. All stories were to be based on scientific and historical facts as we knew them at that time.

Space also meant outer space, intergalactic travel, but again based on understood fact. So no bug-eyed monsters, which I had always thought to be the cheapest form of science fiction.

How wonderful, I thought, if today's humans could find themselves on the shores of England seeing and getting mixed up with Caesar's army in 54 BC, landing to take over the country; be in burning Rome as Nero fiddled; get involved in Europe's tragic Thirty Years war, *et cetera*.

That was the scheme, so how to dress it up?

One thing I was certain of. The space-time machine had to be a very pedestrian-looking, everyday object to shock audiences into not taking the world around them for granted. It must be vast inside but small outside.

Well, how did it get to be on Earth? Who would run it?

To answer both questions I dreamed up the character of a man who is 764 years old; who is senile but with extraordinary flashes of intellectual brilliance. A crotchety old bugger (any kid's grandfather) who had, in a state of terror, escaped in his machine from an advanced civilisation on a distant planet which had been taken over by some unknown enemy. He didn't know who he was any more, and neither did the Earthlings, hence his name, Doctor Who; he didn't know precisely where his home was; he did not fully know how to operate the time-space machine.

In short, he never intended to come to our Earth. In trying to go home he simply pressed the wrong buttons – and kept on pressing the wrong buttons, taking his human passengers backwards and forwards, and in and out of time and space.

Newman put this into a memo to Donald Wilson, head of serials. The serial should be four to six episodes long to minimise the chances of losing the audience, Newman said. And plenty of suspense – a cliff-hanger at the end of every episode.

Wilson was cautiously optimistic. Newman had another idea. The usual serials producers wouldn't get it, so he wanted somebody with a contemporary edge. Specifically, he thought Verity Lambert should have a shot at it. She'd been his production secretary at ABC and was bright, sharp and highly intelligent. She was head-hunted, first to produce *Doctor Who*, and soon disarmed Wilson, who had found her independence of mind rather abrasive at first.

All of them knew science fiction could work; *Quatermass* was unforgettable. Nigel Kneale, who'd written it, disliked the concept of *Doctor Who*, probably because it did not have quite such a strong underlying philosophical thread as *Quatermass;* he turned down an invitation to write for it. Nonetheless, the writers who were brought on board fully understood that what would make *Doctor Who* work was what had brought life to its predecessor: strong, flawed human characters in conflict with an enemy. Or 'plain statements' as Newman said.

Technology had moved on since 1958, and the serial didn't have to go out live. Visual effects were possible, mechanical ones (like the Daleks) were more convincing and reliable, and the Radiophonic Workshop was available to create a memorable signature tune. William Hartnell was recruited to play the part of Doctor Who. Already well known to millions as the sergeant in the TV series *The Army Game*, a part he effectively reprised in *Carry on Sergeant* (the first of the *Carry on* films), Hartnell was perfect for the part of the crotchety, old time traveler. The first ever episode, *A Unearthly Child,* was broadcast on Saturday

23 November, the day after the assassination of President Kennedy. From that moment on, *Doctor Who*, the villainous Daleks, and the wonderful expanding Tardis became cultural reference points for just about everyone in Britain, and the serial ran and ran, thanks to that stroke of genius – a time traveler who could appear in any human form or epoch. After a long break between 1989 and 2005, *Doctor Who* remains the longest-running science fiction serial in the world, and the Doctor himself has been played by eleven different actors.

12

DECEMBER – Capitol Asset

The Cyprus Emergency

Political breakdown had seemed imminent in Cyprus long before December, but order had somehow prevailed until the stand-off between Greek and Turkish Cypriots erupted in violence just before Christmas.

The island had been inhabited since pre-history, and conquered, dominated, indoctrinated and fought over many times. Britain's involvement dated from 1878, when Cyprus was removed from Ottoman governance after the Russio-Turkish War. The British assumed control, although it remained part of the Ottoman Empire. Most of the people who lived there were of Greek heritage, but some – scattered, but mostly in the north – were Turks loyal to the decaying Ottoman Empire.

The Greek Cypriots sought *enosis,* union with Greece. They went on doing so after 1914 when the British annexed Cyprus entirely as a Crown Colony. Agitation for change gathered pace, and became violent, with the prominence after 1955 of EOKA, a pro-*enosis* guerrilla movement led by General Grivas. The popular Greek leader was an Orthodox archbishop, Makarios.

The Turks on the island, however, favoured *taksim* – partition. This plan meant the Greeks would keep to their towns and villages, mostly in the south, and the Turks to theirs, mostly in the north.

The British, who were in charge, wanted to hang on to a useful base in the eastern Mediterranean and leave the Cypriots with a strong framework in which to resolve any differences amicably. In 1960, long negotiations produced proposals that seemed to satisfy the key demands of all three parties.

The British would grant independence and financial assistance to Cyprus, retaining just two small sovereign areas for the RAF and the military. This new independent Cyprus would have a democratic constitution. As the population numbered four Greek Cypriots to every one Turkish Cypriot, representation in government had to reflect that. The Greeks would vote for the president and the Turks for the vice-president; both of them would have the power to veto; and the Cabinet would have seven Greeks and four Turks in it. In big towns, smaller Turkish or Greek enclaves would be formally recognised as municipalities, and would manage their own affairs, in their own interests. Any movement towards either *taksim* or *enosis* was denied under the constitution. Greek and Turkish troops would be stationed on the island to preserve order.

Archbishop Makarios was in exile in the late 1950s, but since he was the only person who could bring the majority Greek population around to this new plan, he was persuaded, after initial opposition, to support it, and in August of 1960 he returned from exile to be the first leader of the Republic of Cyprus. The following year the country joined the United Nations.

Makarios remained under pressure, though, from the military *junta* in Athens and Greek Cypriots who still wanted *enosis*. These locals complained that national efficiency would always founder on obstacles inbuilt in the constition: the Turkish municipalities, for instance (which never in reality took shape), and the need to have a certain number of Turkish representatives in government and public service, and the Turkish power of veto. They wanted what was called the 'Akritas plan', which demanded reform by removal of Turks from public office.

In November of 1963, Makarios announced thirteen amendments to the constitution. On the whole they would put Turkish Cypriots at a disadvantage. There were outbreaks of violence until December, when the Akritas plan was implemented and intervention from mainland Turkey seemed likely. Nicosia erupted when a routine document check by over-zealous police left two Turkish Cypriots dead and a firefight going on between underground organisations. Relationships between the factions visibly broke down and the Turkish Cypriot vice-president, and all his ministers and civil servants, left government on 23 December. An emergency peace conference in London in the New Year failed to reach an agreement. From January, UN peacekeepers were stationed on the island, and the flow of British money stopped. The Turks withdrew to enclaves; the British retained RAF Akrotiri and a barracks, and some land around both; the UN forces stayed; and there was a stalemate. Give or take occasional spats (for instance, invasion by Turkey in the '70s, and the establishment of a buffer zone) this is pretty well the way things remain in Cyprus today.

The Beatles Sign for Capitol Records

All summer, Epstein's people had been trying to get an American record company to back The Beatles. Executives at Decca, Columbia, RCA-Victor and others blanked them time and again. Even Capitol, the Los Angeles-based label, which was actually owned by the EMI group, had turned them down. Capitol had tried before to market British EMI acts like Cliff Richard & The Shadows with zero success. The response from US labels was generally that the name 'The Beatles' sounded funny; they looked peculiar and that the market for this kind of thing in the United States just did not exist.

In September, *She Loves You* was even tried out on a sample of its target audience, in the rate-a-record slot on *Dick Clark's American Bandstand*. It came in at number 73 of 100.

By this time, three Beatles' singles, *Please Please Me*, *From Me to You* and *She Loves You* had already been released in America, albeit by small, regional labels, and had got nowhere. The first two had been put out by the Chicago R&B label Vee-Jay. The label had also agreed to release a re-packaged version of The Beatles' first album, *Please Please Me*, on 22 July 1963, which they had re-titled *Introducing The Beatles*. With insignificant sales of the album and the two preceding singles, Vee-Jay passed over the option of releasing the next single, *She Loves You*. After trying Capitol once more, and being rejected again, The Beatles 'Producer George Martin had finally persuaded the small Philadelphia-based Swan label to take the single, which they released with no great enthusiasm on 16 September 1963. Again the record sold sparingly and Swan, like Vee-Jay before them, decided not to release any further Beatles recordings.

With a new single, *I Want to Hold Your Hand*, recently recorded and scheduled for release in the UK on 23 November, Epstein and Martin made one more attempt to persuade Capitol to release a Beatles single – yet again the answer was a curt 'no'. After this, the fourth rejection from Capitol, Epstein decided to call Capitol's vice-president, Alan Livingstone, personally by long-distance phone call. Livingston later recalled:

I'm sitting in my office one day and I get a call from London from a man named Brian Epstein, who I didn't know. I took the call. And he said, 'I am the personal manager of The Beatles and I don't understand why you won't release them.' And I said, 'Well, frankly, Mr Epstein, I haven't heard them.' And he said, 'Would you please listen and call me back.' And I said, 'OK,' and I called Dexter and said, 'Let me have some Beatles records.' He sent up a few and I listened. I liked them. I thought they were something different. I can't tell you in all honesty I knew how big they'd be, but I thought this is worth a shot. So I called Epstein back and said, 'OK, I'll put them out.' Smart man, Epstein. He said, 'Just a minute, I'm not gonna let you have them unless you spend $40,000,' (that was a pound translation) 'to promote their first single.' You didn't spend $40,000 to promote a single in those days, it was unheard of. For whatever reason, I said 'OK, we'll do it,' and the deal was made.

In those days, record advertising relied on airplay. You put your money where the radio DJs and record store buyers were. The strategy was simple: take care of radio airplay and distribution; the sales will follow. But $40,000 made them get creative. Capitol would use the money to gee up their entire sales force before Christmas and use them to promote '1964 – The Year of The Beatles!'. Major record retailers would be sent bulk copies of a four-page tabloid newspaper called *National Record News* with 'picture after picture and story after story on The Beatles', as their publicity director wrote in a memo. DJs would be get piles of these things to give away, and so, cleverly, would high school students.

Capitol's publicity director wrote the whole thing, from the biographies – including that of Brian Epstein, their manager and the 'fifth Beatle' – to notes about how to achieve 'the distinctive, mushroom-shaped coiffure which has become the group's visual trademark'.

Over a million copies were distributed and the sales force (men, naturally) wore Beatles buttons and Beatles wigs. Stickers and banners told everyone 'The Beatles are Coming!'. *Newsweek* reported that a Capitol salesperson had tried to bribe a cheerleader to hold up a 'The Beatles are Coming!' notice at a game at the Rose Bowl.

Their debut record on Capitol, *I Want to Hold Your Hand/I Saw Her Standing There* was released early, on 26 December. It would be February 1964 before they stepped off the plane. But by then, their records were flying out of the shops. The rest, as they say, is history.

APPENDICES

Appendix 1: 'Non!'

The statement by Charles de Gaulle vetoing British membership of the Common Market was made on 14 January 1963 at a press conference in Paris in response to a question asking him to 'define explicitly France's position towards Britain's entry into the Common Market and the political evolution of Europe'.

De Gaulle's answer was as follows:

That is a very clear question, to which I shall endeavour to reply clearly. I believe that when you talk about economics – and much more so when you practice them – what you say and what you do must conform to realities, because without that you can get into impasses and, sometimes, you even head for ruin.

In this very great affair of the European Economic Community and also in that of eventual adhesion of Great Britain, it is the facts that must first be considered. Feelings, favourable though they might be and are, these feelings cannot be invoked against the real facts of the problem. What are these facts?

The Treaty of Rome was concluded between six Continental states, states which are, economically speaking, one may say, of the same nature. Indeed, whether it be a matter of their industrial or agricultural production, their external exchanges, their habits or their commercial clientele, their living or working conditions, there is between them much more resemblance than difference. Moreover, they are adjacent, they inter-penetrate, they prolong each other through their communications. It is therefore a fact to group them and to link them in such a way that what they have to produce, to buy, to sell, to consume – well, they do produce, buy, sell, consume, in preference in their own ensemble. Doing that is conforming to realities.

Moreover, it must be added that, from the point of view of their economic development, their social progress, their technical capacity, they are, in short, keeping pace. They are marching in similar fashion. It so happens, too, that there is between them no kind of political grievance, no frontier question, no rivalry in domination or power. On the contrary, they are joined in solidarity, especially and primarily, from the aspect of the consciousness they have of defining together an important part of the sources of our civilisation; and also as concerns their security, because they are Continentals and have before them one and the same menace from one extremity to the other of their territorial ensemble. Then, finally, they are in solidarity through the fact that not one among them is bound abroad by any particular political or military accord.

Thus it was psychologically and materially possible to make an economic community of the six, though not without difficulties. When the Treaty of Rome was signed in 1957, it was after long discussions; and when it was concluded, it was necessary – in order to achieve something – that we French put in order our economic, financial, and monetary affairs ... and that was done in 1959. From that moment the community was in principle viable, but then the treaty had to be applied.

This is why when, last January, thought was given to the setting in motion of the second phase of the treaty – in other words a practical start in application – we were led to pose the entry of agriculture into the Common Market as a formal condition. This was finally accepted by our partners but very difficult and very complex arrangements were needed – and some rulings are still outstanding. I note in passing that in this vast undertaking it was the governments that took all the decisions, because authority and responsibility are not to be found elsewhere. But I must say that in preparing and untangling these matters, the Commission in Brussels did some very objective and fitting work. Thereupon Great Britain posed her candidature to the Common Market. She did it after having earlier refused to participate in the communities we are now building, as well as after creating a free trade area with six other states, and, finally, after having – I may well say it (the negotiations held at such length on this subject will be recalled) –

after having put some pressure on the six to prevent a real beginning being made in the application of the Common Market. If England asks in turn to enter, but on her own conditions, this poses without doubt to each of the six states, and poses to England, problems of a very great dimension.

England in effect is insular, she is maritime, she is linked through her exchanges, her markets, her supply lines to the most diverse and often the most distant countries; she pursues essentially industrial and commercial activities, and only slight agricultural ones. She has in all her doings very marked and very original habits and traditions.

In short, the nature, the structure, the very situation (conjuncture) that are England's differ profoundly from those of the Continentals. What is to be done in order that England, as she lives, produces and trades, can be incorporated into the Common Market, as it has been conceived and as it functions? For example, the means by which the people of Great Britain are fed and which are in fact the importation of foodstuffs bought cheaply in the two Americas and in the former dominions, at the same time giving, granting considerable subsidies to English farmers? These means are obviously incompatible with the system which the six have established quite naturally for themselves.

The system of the six – this constitutes making a whole of the agricultural produce of the whole community, in strictly fixing their prices, in prohibiting subsidies, in organising their consumption between all the participants, and in imposing on each of its participants payment to the community of any saving they would achieve in fetching their food from outside instead of eating what the Common Market has to offer. Once again, what is to be done to bring England, as she is, into this system?

One might sometimes have believed that our English friends, in posing their candidature to the Common Market, were agreeing to transform themselves to the point of applying all the conditions which are accepted and practiced by the six. But the question, to know whether Great Britain can now place herself like the Continent and with it inside a tariff which is genuinely common, to renounce all Commonwealth preferences, to cease any pretence that her agriculture be privileged, and, more than that, to treat her engagements with other countries of the free trade area as null and void – that question is the whole question.

It cannot be said that it is yet resolved. Will it be so one day? Obviously only England can answer. The question is even further posed since after England other states which are, I repeat, linked to her through the free trade area, for the same reasons as Britain, would like or wish to enter the Common Market.

It must be agreed that first the entry of Great Britain, and then these states, will completely change the whole of the actions, the agreements, the compensation, the rules which have already been established between the six, because all these states, like Britain, have very important peculiarities. Then it will be another Common Market whose construction ought to be envisaged; but one which would be taken to eleven and then thirteen and then perhaps eighteen would no longer resemble, without any doubt, the one which the six built.

Further, this community, increasing in such fashion, would see itself faced with problems of economic relations with all kinds of other states, and first with the United States. It is to be foreseen that the cohesion of its members, who would be very numerous and diverse, would not endure for long, and that ultimately it would appear as a colossal Atlantic community under American dependence and direction, and which would quickly have absorbed the community of Europe.

It is a hypothesis which in the eyes of some can be perfectly justified, but it is not at all what France is doing or wanted to do – and which is a properly European construction.

Yet it is possible that one day England might manage to transform herself sufficiently to become part of the European community, without restriction, without reserve and preference for anything whatsoever; and in this case the six would open the door to her and France would raise no obstacle, although obviously England's simple participation in the community would considerably change its nature and its volume.

It is possible, too, that England might not yet be so disposed, and it is that which seems to result from the long, long, so long, so long Brussels conversations. But if that is the case, there is nothing there that could be dramatic. First, whatever decision England takes in this matter there is no reason, as far as we are concerned, for the relations we have with her to be changed, and the consideration, the respect which are due to this great state, this great people, will not thereby be in the slightest impaired.

What England has done across the centuries and in the world is recognised as immense. Although there have often been conflicts with France, Britain's glorious participation in the victory which crowned the First World War – we French, we shall always admire it. As for the role England played in the most dramatic and decisive moments of the Second World War, no one has the right to forget it.

In truth, the destiny of the free world, and first of all ours and even that of the United States and Russia, depended in a large measure on the resolution, the solidity and the courage of the English people, as Churchill was able to harness them. Even at the present moment no one can contest British capacity and worth.

Moreover, I repeat, if the Brussels negotiations were shortly not to succeed, nothing would prevent the conclusion between the Common Market and Great Britain of an accord of association designed to safeguard exchanges, and nothing would prevent close relations between England and France from being maintained, nor the pursuit and development of their direct cooperation in all kinds of fields, and notably the scientific, technical and industrial – as the two countries have just proved by deciding to build together the supersonic aircraft Concorde.

Lastly, it is very possible that Britain's own evolution, and the evolution of the universe, might bring the English little by little towards the Continent, whatever delays the achievement might demand, and for my part, that is what I readily believe, and that is why, in my opinion, it will in any case have been a great honour for the British prime minister, for my friend Harold Macmillan, and for his government, to have discerned in good time, to have had enough political courage to have proclaimed it, and to have led their country the first steps down the path which one day, perhaps, will lead it to moor alongside the Continent.

Appendix 2: Football League Tables 1962/63

First Division

		P	W	D	L	F	A	GA	Pts
1	**Everton**	42	25	11	6	84	42	2.000	61
2	Tottenham Hotspur	42	23	9	10	111	62	1.790	55
3	Burnley	42	22	10	10	78	57	1.368	54
4	Leicester City	42	20	12	10	79	53	1.491	52
5	Wolverhampton Wanderers	42	20	10	12	93	65	1.431	50
6	Sheffield Wednesday	42	19	10	13	77	63	1.222	48
7	Arsenal	42	18	10	14	86	77	1.117	46
8	Liverpool	42	17	10	15	71	59	1.203	44
9	Nottingham Forest	42	17	10	15	67	69	0.971	44
10	Sheffield United	42	16	12	14	58	60	0.967	44
11	Blackburn Rovers	42	15	12	15	79	71	1.113	42
12	West Ham United	42	14	12	16	73	69	1.058	40
13	Blackpool	42	13	14	15	58	64	0.906	40
14	West Bromwich Albion	42	16	7	19	71	79	0.899	39
15	Aston Villa	42	15	8	19	62	68	0.912	38
16	Fulham	42	14	10	18	50	71	0.704	38
17	Ipswich Town	42	12	11	19	59	78	0.756	35
18	Bolton Wanderers	42	15	5	22	55	75	0.733	35
19	Manchester United	42	12	10	20	67	81	0.827	34

20	Birmingham City	42	10	13	19	63	90	0.700	33
21	Manchester City	42	10	11	21	58	102	0.569	31
22	Leyton Orient	42	6	9	27	37	81	0.457	21

Second Division

		P	W	D	L	F	A	GA	Pts
1	**Stoke City**	42	20	13	9	73	50	1.460	53
2	Chelsea	42	24	4	14	81	42	1.929	52
3	Sunderland	42	20	12	10	84	55	1.527	52
4	Middlesbrough	42	20	9	13	86	85	1.012	49
5	Leeds United	42	19	10	13	79	53	1.491	48
6	Huddersfield Town	42	17	14	11	63	50	1.260	48
7	Newcastle United	42	18	11	13	79	59	1.339	47
8	Bury	42	18	11	13	51	47	1.085	47
9	Scunthorpe United	42	16	12	14	57	59	0.966	44
10	Cardiff City	42	18	7	17	83	73	1.137	43
11	Southampton	42	17	8	17	72	67	1.075	42
12	Plymouth Argyle	42	15	12	15	76	73	1.041	42
13	Norwich City	42	17	8	17	80	79	1.013	42
14	Rotherham United	42	17	6	19	67	74	0.905	40
15	Swansea Town	42	15	9	18	51	72	0.708	39
16	Portsmouth	42	13	11	18	63	79	0.797	37
17	Preston North End	42	13	11	18	59	74	0.797	37
18	Derby County	42	12	12	18	61	72	0.847	36

19	Grimsby Town	42	11	13	18	55	66	0.833	35
20	Charlton Athletic	42	13	5	24	62	94	0.660	31
21	Walsall	42	11	9	22	53	89	0.596	31
22	Luton Town	42	11	7	24	61	84	0.726	29

Third Division

		P	W	D	L	F	A	GA	Pts
1	**Northampton Town**	46	26	10	10	109	60	1.817	62
2	Swindon Town	46	22	14	10	87	56	1.554	58
3	Port Vale	46	23	8	15	72	58	1.241	54
4	Coventry City	46	18	17	11	83	69	1.203	53
5	Bournemouth & Boscombe Athletic	46	18	16	12	63	46	1.370	52
6	Peterborough United	46	20	11	15	93	75	1.240	51
7	Notts County	46	19	13	14	73	74	0.986	51
8	Southend United	46	19	12	15	75	77	0.974	50
9	Wrexham	46	20	9	17	84	83	1.012	49
10	Hull City	46	19	10	17	74	69	1.072	48
11	Crystal Palace	46	17	13	16	68	58	1.172	47
12	Colchester United	46	18	11	17	73	93	0.785	47
13	Queens Park Rangers	46	17	11	18	85	76	1.118	45
14	Bristol City	46	16	13	17	100	92	1.087	45
15	Shrewsbury Town	46	16	12	18	83	81	1.025	44
16	Millwall	46	15	13	18	82	87	0.943	43
17	Watford	46	17	8	21	82	85	0.965	42

18	Barnsley	46	15	11	20	63	74	0.851	41
19	Bristol Rovers	46	15	11	20	70	88	0.795	41
20	Reading	46	16	8	22	74	78	0.949	40
21	Bradford Park Avenue	46	14	12	20	79	97	0.814	40
22	Brighton & Hove Albion	46	12	12	22	58	84	0.690	36
23	Carlisle United	46	13	9	24	61	89	0.685	35
24	Halifax Town	46	9	12	25	64	106	0.604	30

Fourth Division

		P	W	D	L	F	A	GA	Pts
1	**Brentford**	46	27	8	11	98	64	1.531	62
2	Oldham Athletic	46	24	11	11	95	60	1.583	59
3	Crewe Alexandra	46	24	11	11	86	58	1.483	59
4	Mansfield Town	46	24	9	13	108	69	1.565	57
5	Gillingham	46	22	13	11	71	49	1.449	57
6	Torquay United	46	20	16	10	75	56	1.339	56
7	Rochdale	46	20	11	15	67	59	1.136	51
8	Tranmere Rovers	46	20	10	16	81	67	1.209	50
9	Barrow	46	19	12	15	82	80	1.025	50
10	Workington	46	17	13	16	76	68	1.118	47
11	Aldershot	46	15	17	14	73	69	1.058	47
12	Darlington	46	19	6	21	72	87	0.828	44
13	Southport	46	15	14	17	72	106	0.679	44
14	York City	46	16	11	19	67	62	1.081	43
15	Chesterfield	46	13	16	17	70	64	1.094	42
16	Doncaster Rovers	46	14	14	18	64	77	0.831	42

17	Exeter City	46	16	10	20	57	77	0.740	42
18	Oxford United	46	13	15	18	70	71	0.986	41
19	Stockport County	46	15	11	20	56	70	0.800	41
20	Newport County	46	14	11	21	76	90	0.844	39
21	Chester	46	15	9	22	51	66	0.773	39
22	Lincoln City	46	13	9	24	68	89	0.764	35
23	Bradford City	46	11	10	25	64	93	0.688	32
24	Hartlepools United	46	7	11	28	56	104	0.538	25

Appendix 3: England International Games 1963

FRANCE
1 R. Springett (Sheffield W)
2 J. Armfield (Blackpool)
3 R. Henry (Tottenham)
4 R. Moore (West Ham)
5 B. Labone (Everton)
6 R. Flowers (Wolverhampton)
7 J. Connelly (Burnley)
8 R. Tambling (Chelsea)
9 R. Smith (Tottenham)
10 J. Greaves (Tottenham)
11 R. Charlton (Manchester U)

SCOTLAND
1 G. Banks (Leicester C)
2 J. Armfield (Blackpool)
3 G. Byrne (Liverpool)
4 R. Moore (West Ham U)
5 M. Norman (Tottenham)
6 R. Flowers (Wolverhampton)
7 B. Douglas (Blackburn R)
8 J. Greaves (Tottenham)
9 R. Smith (Tottenham)
10 J. Melia (Southampton)
11 R. Charlton (Manchester U)

PARIS
27 Feb: 2-5
Smith, Tambling

WEMBLEY
6 April: 1-2
Douglas

BRAZIL
1 G. Banks (Leicester C)
2 J. Armfield (Blackpool)
3 R. Wilson (Huddersfield T)
4 G. Milne (Liverpool)
5 M. Norman (Tottenham)
6 R. Moore (West Ham U)
7 B. Douglas (Blackburn R)
8 J. Greaves (Tottenham)
9 R. Smith (Tottenham)
10 G. Eastham (Arsenal)
11 R. Charlton (Manchester U)

CZECHOSLOVAKIA
1 G. Banks (Leicester C)
2 K. Shellito (Chelsea)
3 R. Wilson (Huddersfield T)
4 G. Milne (Liverpool)
5 M. Norman (Tottenham)
6 R. Moore (West Ham U)
7 T. Paine (Southampton)
8 J. Greaves (Tottenham)
9 R. Smith (Tottenham)
10 G. Eastham (Arsenal)
11 R. Charlton (Manchester U)

WEMBLEY
8 May: 1-1
Douglas, Charlton

BRATISLAVA
20 May: 4-2
Greaves (2), Smith

EAST GERMANY
1 G. Banks (Leicester C)
2 J. Armfield (Blackpool)
3 R. Wilson (Huddersfield T)
4 G. Milne (Liverpool)
5 M. Norman (Tottenham)
6 R. Moore (West Ham U)
7 T. Paine (Southampton)
8 R. Hunt (Liverpool)
9 R. Smith (Tottenham)
10 G. Eastham (Arsenal)
11 R. Charlton (Manchester U)

SWITZERLAND
1 R. Springett (Sheffield W)
2 J. Armfield (Blackpool)
3 R. Wilson (Huddersfield T)
4 A. Kay (Everton)
5 M. Norman (Tottenham)
6 R. Flowers (Wolverhampton)
7 B. Douglas (Blackburn Rovers)
8 J. Greaves (Tottenham)
9 G. Byrne (Liverpool)
10 J. Melia (Southampton)
11 R. Charlton (Manchester U)

LEIPZIG
2 June: 2-1
Hunt, Charlton

BASLE
5 June: 8-1
Charlton (3), Byrne (2),
Douglas, Kay, Melia

WALES
1 G. Banks (Leicester C)
2 J. Armfield (Blackpool)
3 R. Wilson (Huddersfield T)
4 G. Milne (Liverpool)
5 M. Norman (Tottenham)
6 R. Moore (West Ham U)
7 T. Paine (Southampton)
8 J. Greaves (Tottenham)
9 R. Smith (Tottenham)
10 G. Eastham (Arsenal)
11 R. Charlton (Manchester U)

REST OF THE WORLD
1 G. Banks (Leicester C)
2 J. Armfield (Blackpool)
3 R. Wilson (Huddersfield T)
4 G. Milne (Liverpool)
5 M. Norman (Tottenham)
6 R. Moore (West Ham U)
7 T. Paine (Southampton)
8 J. Greaves (Tottenham)
9 R. Smith (Tottenham)
10 G. Eastham (Arsenal)
11 R. Charlton (Manchester U)

CARDIFF
12 Oct: 4-0
Greaves, Smith (2),
Charlton

WEMBLEY
23 Oct: 2-1
Paine, Greaves

NORTHERN IRELAND
1 G. Banks (Leicester C)
2 J. Armfield (Blackpool)
3 R. Thompson (Liverpool)
4 G. Milne (Liverpool)
5 M. Norman (Tottenham)
6 R. Moore (West Ham U)
7 T. Paine (Southampton)
8 J. Greaves (Tottenham)
9 R. Smith (Tottenham)
10 G. Eastham (Arsenal)
11 R. Charlton (Manchester U)

WEMBLEY
20 Nov: 8-3
Greaves (4), Paine (3),
Smith

Appendix 4: British No. 1 Singles 1963*

Date	Song	Artist	Label
5 January	*Dance On*	The Shadows	Columbia
12 January	*Dance On*	The Shadows	Columbia
19 January	*Dance On*	The Shadows	Columbia
26 January	*Diamonds*	Jet Harris & Tony Meehan	Decca
2 February	*Diamonds*	Jet Harris & Tony Meehan	Decca
9 February	*Diamonds*	Jet Harris & Tony Meehan	Decca
16 February	Diamonds	Jet Harris & Tony Meehan	Decca
23 February	*Please Please Me*	The Beatles	Parlophone
2 March	*Please Please Me*	The Beatles	Parlophone
9 March	*Summer Holiday*	Cliff Richard	Columbia
16 March	*Summer Holiday*	Cliff Richard	Columbia
23 March	*Summer Holiday*	Cliff Richard	Columbia
30 March	*Foot Tapper*	The Shadows	Columbia
6 April	*How Do You Do It?*	Gerry & The Pacemakers	Columbia
13 April	*How Do You Do It?*	Gerry & The Pacemakers	Columbia
20 April	*How Do You Do It?*	Gerry & The Pacemakers	Columbia
27 April	*From Me to You*	The Beatles	Parlophone
4 May	*From Me to You*	The Beatles	Parlophone
11 May	*From Me to You*	The Beatles	Parlophone
18 May	*From Me to You*	The Beatles	Parlophone
25 May	*From Me to You*	The Beatles	Parlophone
1 June	*Do You Want to Know a Secret?*	Billy J. Kramer	Parlophone
8 June	*Do You Want to Know a Secret?*	Billy J. Kramer	Parlophone
15 June	*I Like It*	Gerry & The Pacemakers	Columbia
22 June	*I Like It*	Gerry & The Pacemakers	Columbia
29 June	*I Like It*	Gerry & The Pacemakers	Columbia
6 July	*I Like It*	Gerry & The Pacemakers	Columbia
13 July	*Confessin'*	Frank Ifield	Columbia

*Data from New Musical Express in UK and Billboard in the USA

20 July	*Confessin'*	Frank Ifield	Columbia
27 July	Confessin'	Frank Ifield	Columbia
3 August	*Sweets for My Sweet*	The Searchers	Pye
10 August	*Sweets for My Sweet*	The Searchers	Pye
17 August	*Sweets for My Sweet*	The Searchers	Pye
24 August	*Bad to Me*	Billy J. Kramer	Parlophone
31 August	*Bad to Me*	Billy J. Kramer	Parlophone
7 September	*She Loves You*	The Beatles	Parlophone
14 September	*She Loves You*	The Beatles	Parlophone
21 September	*She Loves You*	The Beatles	Parlophone
28 September	*She Loves You*	The Beatles	Parlophone
5 October	*Do You Love Me?*	Brian Poole/Tremeloes	Decca
12 October	*Do You Love Me?*	Brian Poole/Tremeloes	Decca
19 October	*Do You Love Me?*	Brian Poole/Tremeloes	Decca
26 October	*You'll Never Walk Alone*	Gerry & The Pacemakers	Columbia
2 November	*You'll Never Walk Alone*	Gerry & The Pacemakers	Columbia
9 November	*You'll Never Walk Alone*	Gerry & The Pacemakers	Columbia
16 November	*You'll Never Walk Alone*	Gerry & THe Pacemakers	Columbia
23 November	*She Loves You*	The Beatles	Parlophone
30 November	*She Loves You*	The Beatles	Parlophone
7 December	*I Want to Hold Your Hand*	The Beatles	Parlophone
14 December	*I Want to Hold Your Hand*	The Beatles	Parlophone
21 December	*I Want to Hold Your Hand*	The Beatles	Parlophone
28 December	*I Want to Hold Your Hand*	The Beatles	Parlophone

Appendix 5: American No. 1 Singles 1963*

Date	Song	Artist	Label
5 January	Telstar	The Tornadoes	London
12 January	Go Away Little Girl	Steve Lawrence	Columbia
19 January	Go Away Little Girl	Steve Lawrence	Columbia
26 January	Walk Right In	The Rooftop Singers	Vanguard
2 February	Walk Right In	The Roof top Singers	Vanguard
9 February	Hey Paula	Paul & Paula	Philips
16 February	Hey Paula	Paul & Paula	Philips
23 February	Hey Paula	Paul & Paula	Philips
2 March	Walk Like a Man	The Four Seasons	Vee Jay
9 March	Walk Like a Man	The Four Seasons	Vee Jay
16 March	Walk Like a Man	The Four Seasons	Vee Jay
23 March	Our Day Will Come	Ruby & Romantics	Kapp
30 March	He's So Fine	Chiffons	Laurie
6 April	He's So Fine	Chiffons	Laurie
13 April	He's So Fine	Chiffons	Laurie
20 April	He's So Fine	Chiffons	Laurie
27 April	I Will Follow Him	Little Peggie March	RCA
4 May	I Will Follow Him	Little Peggie March	RCA
11 May	I Will Follow Him	Little Peggie March	RCA
18 May	If You Wanna Be Happy	Jimmy Soul	SPQR
25 May	If You Wanna Be Happy	Jimmy Soul	SPQR
1 June	It's My Party	Leslie Gore	Mercury
7 June	It's My Party	Leslie Gore	Mercury
15 June	Sukiyaki	Kyu Sakamoto	Capitol
21 June	Sukiyaki	Kyu Sakamoto	Capitol
28 June	Sukiyaki	Kyu Sakamoto	Capitol
6 July	Easier Said Than Done	The Essex	Roulette
13 July	Easier Said Than Done	The Essex	Roulette
20 July	Surf City	Jan & Dean	Liberty
27 July	Surf City	Jan & Dean	Liberty
3 August	So Much In Love	The Tymes	Parkway

10 August	*Fingertips*	Little Stevie Wonder	Tamla
17 August	*Fingertips*	Little Stevie Wonder	Tamla
24 August	Fingertips	Little Stevie Wonder	Tamla
31 August	*My Boyfriend's Back*	The Angels	Smash
7 September	*My Boyfriend's Back*	The Angels	Smash
14 September	*My Boyfriend's Back*	The Angels	Smash
21 September	*Blue Velvet*	Bobby Vinton	Epic
28 September	*Blue Velvet*	Bobby Vinton	Epic
5 October	*Blue Velvet*	Bobby Vinton	Epic
12 October	*Sugar Shack*	Jimmy Gilmer	Dot
19 October	*Sugar Shack*	Jimmy Gilmer	Dot
26 October	*Sugar Shack*	Jimmy Gilmer	Dot
2 November	*Sugar Shack*	Jimmy Gilmer	Dot
9 November	*Sugar Shack*	Jimmy Gilmer	Dot
16 November	*Deep Purple*	Nino Tempo & April Stevens	Atco
23 November	*I'm Leaving It Up To You*	Dale & Grace	Montel
7 December	*Dominique*	The Singing Nun	Philips
14 December	*Dominique*	The Singing Nun	Philips
21 December	*Dominique*	The Singing Nun	Philips
28 December	*Dominique*	The Singing Nun	Philips

Appendix 6: The Unspoken Speech

Had President John F. Kennedy not been assassinated at 12.30 p.m. on 22 November 1963 in Dallas, Texas, he would have proceeded to the Texas Trade Mart where he was to have given one of two keynote speeches that day. The two speeches would effectively set out the themes for his 1964 campaign for re-election to the White House.

The 'unspoken' speeches had already been written and rehearsed, and have only recently been made available by the Kennedy Library:

Speech at the Dallas Trade Mart by President John F. Kennedy, 22 November 1963

I am honoured to have this invitation to address the annual meeting of the Dallas Citizens Council, joined by the members of the Dallas Assembly – and pleased to have this opportunity to salute the Graduate Research Center of the Southwest.

It is fitting that these two symbols of Dallas progress are united in the sponsorship of this meeting. For they represent the best qualities, I am told, of leadership and learning in this city – and leadership and learning are indispensable to each other. The advancement of learning depends on community leadership for financial and political support and the products of that learning, in turn, are essential to the leadership's hopes for continued progress and prosperity. It is not a coincidence that those communities possessing the best in research and graduate facilities from MIT to Cal Tech tend to attract the new and growing industries. I congratulate those of you here in Dallas who have recognized these basic facts through the creation of the unique and forward-looking Graduate Research Center.

This link between leadership and learning is not only essential at the community level. It is even more indispensable in world affairs. Ignorance and misinformation can handicap the progress of a city or a company, but they can, if allowed to prevail in foreign policy, handicap this country's security. In a world of complex and continuing problems, in a world full of frustrations and irritations, America's leadership must be guided by the lights of learning and reason or else those who confuse rhetoric with reality and the plausible with the possible will gain the popular ascendancy with their seemingly swift and simple solutions to every world problem.

There will always be dissident voices heard in the land, expressing opposition without alternatives, finding fault but never favour, perceiving gloom on every side and seeking influence without responsibility. Those voices are inevitable.

But today other voices are heard in the land – voices preaching doctrines wholly unrelated to reality, wholly unsuited to the sixties, doctrines which apparently assume that words will suffice without weapons, that vituperation is as good as victory and that peace is a sign of weakness. At a time when the national debt is steadily being reduced in terms of its burden on our economy, they see that debt as the greatest single threat to our security. At a time when we are steadily reducing the number of Federal employees serving every thousand citizens, they fear those supposed hordes of civil servants far more than the actual hordes of opposing armies.

We cannot expect that everyone, to use the phrase of a decade ago, will 'talk sense to the American people'. But we can hope that fewer people will listen to nonsense. And the notion that this Nation is headed for defeat through deficit, or that strength is but a matter of slogans is nothing but just plain nonsense.

I want to discuss with you today the status of our strength and our security because this question clearly calls for the most responsible qualities of leadership and the most enlightened products of scholarship. For this Nation's strength and security are not easily or cheaply obtained, nor are they quickly and simply explained. There are many kinds of strength and no one kind will suffice. Overwhelming nuclear strength cannot stop a guerrilla war. Formal pacts of alliance cannot stop internal subversion. Displays of material wealth cannot stop the disillusionment of diplomats subjected to discrimination.

Above all, words alone are not enough. The United States is a peaceful nation. And where our strength and determination are clear, our words need merely to convey conviction, not belligerence. If we are strong, our strength will speak for itself. If we are weak, words will be of no help.

I realize that this Nation often tends to identify turning-points in world affairs with the major addresses which preceded them. But it was not the Monroe Doctrine that kept all Europe away from this hemisphere – it was the strength of the British fleet and the width of the Atlantic Ocean. It was not General Marshall's speech at Harvard which kept Communism out of Western Europe – it was the strength and stability made possible by our military and economic assistance.

In this administration also it has been necessary at times to issue specific warnings – warnings that we could not stand by and watch the Communists conquer Laos by force, or intervene in the Congo, or swallow West Berlin, or maintain offensive missiles on Cuba. But while our goals were at least temporarily obtained in these and other instances, our successful defense of freedom was due not to the words we used, but to the strength we stood ready to use on behalf of the principles we stand ready to defend.

This strength is composed of many different elements, ranging from the most massive deterrents to the most subtle influences. And all types of strength are needed – no one kind could do the job alone. Let us take a moment, therefore, to review this Nation's progress in each major area of strength.

I.

First, as Secretary McNamara made clear in his address last Monday, the strategic nuclear power of the United States has been so greatly modernized and expanded in the last 1,000 days, by the rapid production and deployment of the most modern missile systems, that any and all potential aggressors are clearly confronted now with the impossibility of strategic victory —and the certainty of total destruction – if by reckless attack they should ever force upon us the necessity of a strategic reply.

In less than 3 years, we have increased by 50 per cent the number of Polaris submarines scheduled to be in force by the next fiscal year, increased by more than 70 per cent our total Polaris purchase program, increased by more than 75 per cent our Minuteman purchase program, increased by 50 per cent the portion of our strategic bombers on 15-minute alert, and increased by 2 per cent the total number of nuclear weapons available in our strategic alert forces. Our security is further enhanced by the steps we have taken regarding these weapons to improve the speed and certainty of their response, their readiness at all times to respond, their ability to survive an attack, and their ability to be carefully controlled and directed through secure command operations.

But the lessons of the last decade have taught us that freedom cannot be defended by strategic nuclear power alone. We have, therefore, in the last 3 years accelerated the development and deployment of tactical nuclear weapons, and increased by 60 per cent the tactical nuclear forces deployed in Western Europe.

Nor can Europe or any other continent rely on nuclear forces alone, whether they are strategic or tactical. We have radically improved the readiness of our conventional forces increased by 45 per cent the number of combat ready Army divisions, increased by 100 per cent the procurement of modern Army weapons and equipment, increased by 100 per cent our ship construction, conversion, and modernization program, increased by 100 per cent our procurement of tactical aircraft, increased by 30 per cent the number of tactical air squadrons, and increased the strength of the Marines. As last month's 'Operation Big Lift' which originated here in Texas showed so clearly, this Nation is prepared as never before to move substantial numbers of men in surprisingly little time to advanced positions anywhere in the world. We have increased by 175 per cent the procurement of airlift aircraft, and we have already achieved a 75 per cent increase in our existing strategic airlift capability. Finally, moving beyond the traditional roles of our military forces, we have achieved an increase of nearly 600 per cent in our special forces – those forces that are prepared to work with our allies and friends against the guerrillas, saboteurs, insurgents and assassins who threaten freedom in a less direct but equally dangerous manner.

But American military might should not and need not stand alone against the ambitions of international Communism. Our security and strength, in the last analysis, directly depend on the security and strength of others, and that is why our military and economic assistance plays such a key role in enabling those who live on the periphery of the Communist world to maintain their independence of choice. Our assistance to these nations can be painful, risky and costly, as is true in South East Asia today. But we dare not weary of the task. For our assistance makes possible the stationing of 3-5 million allied troops along the Communist frontier at one-tenth the cost of maintaining a comparable number of American soldiers. A successful Communist breakthrough in these areas, necessitating direct United States intervention, would cost us several times as much as our entire foreign aid program, and might cost us heavily in American lives as well.

About 70 per cent of our military assistance goes to nine key countries located on or near the borders of the Communist bloc – nine countries confronted directly or indirectly with the threat of Communist aggression – Vietnam, Free China, Korea, India, Pakistan, Thailand, Greece, Turkey, and Iran. No one of these countries possesses on its own the resources to maintain the forces which our own Chiefs of Staff think needed in the common interest. Reducing our efforts to train, equip, and assist their armies can only encourage Communist penetration and require in time the increased overseas deployment of American combat forces. And reducing the economic help needed to bolster these nations that undertake to help defend freedom can have the same disastrous result. In short, the $50 billion we spend each year on our own defence could well be ineffective without the $4 billion required for military and economic assistance.

Our foreign aid program is not growing in size, it is, on the contrary, smaller now than in previous years. It has had its weaknesses, but we have undertaken to correct them. And the proper way of treating weaknesses is to replace them with strength, not to increase those weaknesses by emasculating essential programs. Dollar for dollar, in or out of government, there is no better form of investment in our national security than our much-abused foreign aid program. We cannot afford to lose it. We can afford to maintain it. We can surely afford, for example, to do as much for our 19 needy neighbours of Latin America as the Communist bloc is sending to the island of Cuba alone.

I have spoken of strength largely in terms of the deterrence and resistance of aggression and attack. But, in today's world, freedom can be lost without a shot being fired, by ballots as well as bullets. The success of our leadership is dependent upon respect for our mission in the world as well as our missiles on a clearer recognition of the virtues of freedom as well as the evils of tyranny.

That is why our Information Agency has doubled the shortwave broadcasting power of the Voice of America and increased the number of broadcasting hours by 30 per cent, increased Spanish language broadcasting to Cuba and Latin America from 1 to 9 hours a day, increased seven-fold to more than 3-5 million copies the number of American books being translated and published for Latin American readers, and taken a host of other steps to carry our message of truth and freedom to all the far corners of the earth.

And that is also why we have regained the initiative in the exploration of outer space, making an annual effort greater than the combined total of all space activities undertaken during the fifties, launching more than 130 vehicles into earth orbit, putting into actual operation valuable weather and communications satellites, and making it clear to all that the United States of America has no intention of finishing second in space.

This effort is expensive – but it pays its own way, for freedom and for America. For there is no longer any fear in the free world that a Communist lead in space will become a permanent assertion of supremacy and the basis of military superiority. There is no longer any doubt about the strength and skill of American science, American industry, American education, and the American free enterprise system. In short, our national space effort represents a great gain in, and a great resource of, our national strength – and both Texas and Texans are contributing greatly to this strength.

Finally, it should be clear by now that a nation can be no stronger abroad than she is at home. Only an America which practices what it preaches about equal rights and social justice will be respected by those whose choice affects our future. Only in America which has fully educated its citizens is fully capable of tackling the complex problems and perceiving the hidden dangers of the world in which we live. And only an America which is growing and prospering economically can sustain the worldwide defenses of freedom, while demonstrating to all concerned the opportunities of our system and society.

It is clear, therefore, that we are strengthening our security as well as our economy by our recent record increases in national income and output - by surging ahead of most of Western Europe in the rate of business expansion and the margin of corporate profits, by maintaining a more stable level of prices than almost any of our overseas competitors, and by cutting personal and corporate income taxes by some $11 billion, as I have proposed, to assure this Nation of the longest and strongest expansion in our peacetime economic history.

This Nation's total output which 3 years ago was at the $500 billion mark will soon pass $600 billion, for a record rise of over $100 billion in 3 years. For the first time in history we have 70 million men and women at work. For the first time in history average factory earnings have exceeded $100 a week. For the first time in history corporation profits after taxes – which have risen 43 per cent in less than 3 years – have an annual level of $27.4 billion.

My friends and fellow citizens: I cite these facts and figures to make it clear that America today is stronger than ever before. Our adversaries have not abandoned their ambitions, our dangers have not diminished, our vigilance cannot be relaxed. But now we have the military, the scientific, and the economic strength to do whatever must be done for the preservation and promotion of freedom.

That strength will never be used in pursuit of aggressive ambitions it will always be used in pursuit of peace. It will never be used to promote provocations it will always be used to promote the peaceful settlement of disputes.

We in this country, in this generation, are by destiny rather than choice the watchmen on the walls of world freedom. We ask, therefore, that we may be worthy of our power and responsibility, that we may exercise our strength with wisdom and restraint, and that we may achieve in our time and for all time the ancient vision of 'peace on earth, good will toward men.' That must always be our goal, and the righteousness of our cause must always underlie our strength. For as was written long ago: 'except the Lord keep the city, the watchman wake but in vain.'

Courtesy of the John Fitzgerald Kennedy Library, Boston, Massachusetts

Appendix 7: The Macmillan Government

Position	Name	Dates
Prime Minister	H. Macmillan	10 Jan 57 – 13 Oct 63
First Secretary of State	R. Butler	13 Jul 62 – 13 Oct 63
Lord President of the Council	Marquis of Salisbury	13 Jan 57 – 29 Mar 57
	Earl Home	29 Mar 57 – 17 Sep 57
	Viscount Hailsham	17 Sep 57 – 14 Oct 59
	Earl Home	14 Oct 59 – 27 Jul 60
	Viscount Hailsham	27 Jul 60 – 13 Oct 63
Lord Chancellor	Viscount Kilmuir	14 Jan 57 – 13 Jul 62
	Lord Dilhorne	13 Jul 62 – 13 Oct 63
Lord Privy Seal	R. Butler	13 Jan 57 – 14 Oct 59
	Viscount Hailsham	14 Oct 59 – 27 Jul 60
	E. Heath	27 Jul 60 – 13 Oct 63
Chancellor of the Exchequer	P. Thorneycroft	13 Jan 57 – 6 Jan 58
	D. Heathcoat Amory	6 Jan 58 – 27 Jul 60
	S. Lloyd	27 Jul 60 – 13 Jul 62
	R. Maudling	13 Jul 62 – 13 Oct 63
Secretary of State for Foreign Affairs	S. Lloyd	14 Jan 57 – 27 Jul 60
	Earl Home	27 Jul 60 – 13 Oct 63
Secretary of State for Home Affairs	R. Butler	13 Jan 57 – 13 Jul 62
	H. Brooke	13 Jul 62 – 13 Oct 63
Minister of Agriculture and Fisheries	D. Heathcoat Amory	14 Jan 57 – 6 Jan 58
	J. Hare	6 Jan 58 – 27 Jul 60
	C. Soames	27 Jul 60 – 13 Oct 63
Secretary of State for Aviation	D. Sandys	14 Oct 59 – 27 Jul 60
	P. Thorneycroft	27 Jul 60 – 16 Jul 62
Secretary of State for the Colonies	A. Lennox Boyd	14 Jan 57 – 14 Oct 59
	I. MacLeod	14 Oct 59 – 9 Oct 61
	R. Maudling	9 Oct 61 – 13 Jul 62
	D. Sandys	13 Jul 62 – 13 Oct 63
Secretary of State for Commonwealth Relations	Earl Home	14 Jan 57 – 27 Jul 60
	D. Sandys	27 Jul 60 – 13 Jul 62

Minister for Defence	D. Sandys	13 Jan 57 – 14 Oct 59
	P. Thorneycroft	14 Oct 59 – 13 Oct 63
Minister of Education	Viscount Hailsham	13 Jan 57 – 17 Sep 57
	G. Lloyd	17 Sep 57 – 14 Oct 59
	Sir D. Eccles	14 Oct 59 – 13 Oct 63
Minister of Health	E. Powell	13 Jul 62 – 13 Oct 63
Minister for Housing	H. Brooke	13 Jan 57 – 9 Oct 61
	C. Hill	9 Oct 61 – 13 Jul 62
	Sir K. Joseph	13 Jul 62 – 13 Oct 63
Minister of Labour and National Service	I. MacLeod	14 Jan 57 – 14 Oct 59
	E. Heath	14 Oct 59 – 27 Jul 60
	J. Hare	27 Jul 60 – 13 Oct 63
Chancellor of the Duchy of Lancaster	C. Hill	13 Jan 57 – 9 Oct 61
	I. MacLeod	9 Oct 61 – 13 Oct 63
Paymaster-General	R. Maudling	17 Sep 57 – 14 Oct 59
	Lord Mills	14 Oct 59 – 9 Oct 61
	H. Brooke	9 Oct 61 – 13 Jul 62
	J. Boyd-Carpenter	13 Jul 62 – 13 Oct 63
Minister without Portfolio	Lord Mills	9 Oct 61 – 14 Jul 62
	W. Deedes	13 Jul 62 – 13 Oct 63
Minister for Power	Lord Mills	13 Jan 57 – 14 Oct 59
Minister for Science	Viscount Hailsham	14 Oct 59 – 13 Oct 63
Secretary of State for Scotland	J. MacLay	13 Jan 57 – 13 Jul 62
	M. Noble	13 Jul 62 – 13 Oct 63
President of the Board of Trade	Sir D. Eccles	13 Jan 57 – 14 Oct 59
	R. Maudling	14 Oct 59 – 9 Oct 61
	F. Erroll	9 Oct 61 – 13 Oct 63
Minister of Transport and Civil Aviation	H. Watkinson	13 Jan 57 – 14 Oct 59
Minister for Transport	E. Marples	14 Oct 59 – 13 Oct 63

Appendix 8: The Douglas Home Government

Position	Name	Dates
Prime Minister	Sir A. Douglas Home	18 Oct 63 – 16 Oct 64
Lord President of the Council	Viscount Hailsham	18 Oct 63 – 16 Oct 64
Lord Chancellor	Lord Dilhorne	13 Oct 63 – 16 Oct 64
Lord Privy Seal	S. Lloyd	20 Oct 63 – 16 Oct 64
Chancellor of the Exchequer	R. Maudling	18 Oct 63 – 16 Oct 64
Secretary of State for Foreign Affairs	R. Butler	20 Oct 63 – 16 Oct 64
Secretary of State for Home Affairs	H. Brooke	18 Oct 63 – 16 Oct 64
Minister of Agriculture and Fisheries	C. Soames	18 Oct 63 – 16 Oct 64
Secretary of State for the Colonies	D. Sandys	18 Oct 63 – 16 Oct 64
Minister for Defence	P. Thorneycroft	18 Oct 63 – 16 Oct 64
Minister of Education	Sir E. Boyle	18 Oct 63 – 1 Apr 64
	Q. Hogg	1 Apr 64 – 16 Oct 64
Minister of State	Sir E. Boyle	1 Apr 64 – 16 Oct 64
Minister of Health	A. Barber	20 Oct 63 – 16 Oct 64
Minister for Housing	Sir K. Joseph	18 Oct 63 – 16 Oct 64
Minister of Labour	J. Godber	20 Oct 63 – 16 Oct 64
Chancellor of the Duchy of Lancaster	Viscount Blakenham	20 Oct 63 – 16 Oct 64
Paymaster-General	J. Boyd-Carpenter	18 Oct 63 – 18 Oct 64
Minister without Portfolio	W. Deedes	18 Oct 63 – 16 Oct 64
	Lord Carrington	20 Oct 63 – 16 Oct 64
Minister for Power	F. Erroll	20 Oct 63 – 16 Oct 64
Minister for Science	Viscount Hailsham	18 Oct 63 – 16 Oct 64
Secretary of State for Scotland	M. Noble	18 Oct 63 – 16 Oct 64
President of the Board of Trade	E. Heath	20 Oct 63 – 16 Oct 64
Minister for Transport	E. Marples	18 Oct 63 – 16 Oct 64
Minister for Works	G. Rippon	20 Oct 63 – 16 Oct 64

Appendix 9: The Great Train Robbers

Following the trial of those Great Train Robbers who had been arrested in 1963, the judge, Justice Edmund Davies, passed sentence on all prisoners who had been found guilty one by one:

Roger Cordrey

Roger John Cordrey, you are the first to be sentenced out of certainly eleven greedy men whom hope of gain allured. You and your co-accused have been convicted of complicity, in one way or another, of a crime which in its impudence and enormity is the first of its kind in this country. I propose to do all within my power to ensure it will also be the last of its kind; outrageous conduct constitutes an intolerable menace to the wellbeing of society.

Let us clear out of the way any romantic notions of dare-devilry. This is nothing less than a sordid crime of violence inspired by vast greed. The motive of greed is obvious. As to violence, anybody who has seen that nerve-shattered engine driver can have no doubt of the terrifying effect on law-abiding citizens of a concerted assault by masked and armed robbers in lonely darkness. To deal with this case leniently would be a positively evil thing. When grave crime is committed it calls for grave punishment, not for the purpose of mere retribution but so that others similarly tempted shall be brought to the sharp realisation that crime does not pay and that the crime is most certainly not worth even the most alluring candle. As the higher the price the greater the temptation, potential criminals who may be dazzled by the enormity of the price must be taught that the punishment they risk will be proportionately greater.

I therefore find myself faced with the unenviable duty of pronouncing grave sentences. You, Cordrey, and the other accused vary widely in intelligence, strength of personality, in antecedent history, in age and in many other ways. Some convicted on this indictment have absolutely clean characters up to the present. Some have previous convictions of a comparatively minor character and others have previous convictions of gravity which could now lead to sentences of corrective training or even of preventive detention.

To some the degradation to which you have all now sunk will bring consequences vastly more cruel than to the other. I have anxiously sought to bear in mind everything that has been urged on behalf of all the accused by your learned Counsel, to whom I am so greatly indebted, but whatever the past of a particular accused and whatever his position, all else pales into insignificance in the light of his present offences. Furthermore, the evidence, or rather the lack of it, renders it impossible to determine exactly what part was played by each of the eleven accused convicted of the larger conspiracy or the eight convicted of the actual robbery. I therefore propose, after mature deliberation, to treat you all in the same manner with but two exceptions.

You, Cordrey, are the first of the exceptions. On your own confession you stand convicted on the first count of conspiracy to rob the mail and on counts 3, 4 and 5 of receiving in all nearly £141,000 of the stolen money, but when arrested you immediately gave information to the police which enabled them to put their hands on nearly £80,000 and the remainder was eventually recovered. Furthermore, at the outset of this trial you confessed your guilt and I feel I should give recognition to that fact in determining your sentence. I do this because it is greatly in the public interest that the guilty should confess their guilt. This massive trial is the best demonstration of the truth of that proposition. In respect of the four counts you must go to prison for concurrent terms of 20 years.

William Boal

William Gerald Boal, you, who are substantially the oldest of the accused, have been convicted of conspiracy to rob the mail and of armed robbery itself. You have expressed no repentance for your wrong-doing, indeed, you continue to assert your innocence but you beg for mercy. I propose to extend to you some measure of mercy and I do it on two grounds. Firstly, on account of your age, you being a man of 50 and, secondly, because, having seen and heard you, I cannot believe that you were one of the originators of the conspiracy or that you played a very dynamic part in it or in the robbery itself. Detective Superintendent Fewtrell has confirmed me in that view of you which I had already formed, but your participation in any degree nevertheless remains a matter of extreme gravity. In the light of these considerations the concurrent sentences you will serve are, upon the first count, 21 years and upon the second count 24 years.

Charles Wilson

Charles Frederick Wilson, you have been convicted of conspiracy to rob the mail and of armed robbery. No one has said less than you throughout this long trial. Indeed, I doubt if you have spoken half a dozen words. Certainly no word of repentance has been expressed by you. I bear in mind those matters which your learned Counsel has urged upon your behalf, but my duty, as I conceive it, is clear. If you or any of the order accused still to be dealt with had assisted justice that would have told strongly in your favour, but you have not. The consequences of this outrageous crime is that the vast booty of something like £2½ million still remains almost entirely unrecovered. It would be an affront to the public weal that any of you should be at liberty in anything like the near future to enjoy any of those ill-gotten gains.

Accordingly, it is no spirit of mere retribution that I propose to secure that such an opportunity will be denied all of you for an extremely long time. Nevertheless, the plea of Mr Wilfred Fordham for a gleam of light at the end of the long dark tunnel to be left for his client, is a plea I intend to heed in respect of all of you. On the first count you will go to prison for 25 years and on the second count you will be sentenced to a concurrent term of 30 years.

Ronald Biggs

Ronald Arthur Biggs, yesterday you were convicted of both the first and second counts of this indictment. Your learned Counsel has urged that you had no special talent and you were plainly not an originator of the conspiracy. Those and all other submissions I bear in mind, but the truth is that I do not know when you entered the conspiracy or what part you played. What I do know is that you are a specious and facile liar and you have this week, in this court, perjured yourself time and again, but I add not a day to your sentence on that account. Your previous record qualifies you to be sentenced to preventive detention; that I shall not do. Instead, the sentence of the court upon you in respect of the first count is one of 25 years' imprisonment and in respect of the second count, 30 years' imprisonment. Those sentences to be served concurrently.

Thomas Wisbey

Thomas William Wisbey, you stand convicted on the first and second counts. Your previous record qualifies you for corrective training but any such sentence is plainly out of the question in the present circumstances. In your case again I have no evidence upon which I can measure the degree or quality of your participation in the vast criminal enterprise which has given rise to this trial. Your learned Counsel has urged that you are plainly not a dominant character and that the part you played was subsidiary and was perhaps connected with transport matters. You yourself have thrown no light upon that or upon any other topic and you have not sought to mollify the court by any admission of repentance. The sentences upon you are concurrent sentences. In respect of the first count, 25 years' imprisonment and in respect of the second count, 30 years' imprisonment.

Robert Welch

Robert Alfred Welch, you have been convicted on the first and second counts of this indictment. Your counsel has urged upon me that there is no evidence of any sudden flowing of money into your pockets or as to when you joined the conspiracy or what you actually did. These and all matters urged in mitigation and your antecedents, I have sought faithfully to bear in mind. The sentence of the court upon you is that on the first count you go to prison for 25 years and upon the second count you go to prison for 30 years. Those sentences will be concurrent.

James Hussey

James Hussey, you have been convicted on the first and second counts of this indictment. You have previous convictions of gravity, including two involving substantial violence. On the other hand, I accept that as a son you are warm-hearted and it is obvious you have qualities of personality and intelligence which you might have put to very good stead. I balance these and all other matters to the best of my ability and having done so the concurrent sentences that you will serve are, on the first count, 25 years' imprisonment and on the second count, 30 years.

Roy James

Roy John James, you have been convicted on both the first and second courts. You are the only one out of the accused in respect of whom it has been proved that you actually received a substantial part of the stolen moneys. On your arrest you still had in your possession over £12,000 which I have no doubt was the result of exchange out of the original stolen moneys received by you. I entertain no doubt that the original sum you received substantially exceeded that figure. Your record in the past is a bad one and corrective training seems to have done you little or no good. Yet you have ability of a kind which would have assured you an honest livelihood of substantial proportion; for in a very short space of time you had, as your learned Counsel has said, brilliant and meteoric success as a racing driver. I strongly suspect that it was your known talent as a driver which enabled you to play an important part in the perpetration of this grave crime. It may be, as you say, that you personally have never resorted to physical violence, but you nevertheless stand convicted of participating with others in armed robbery and for that you must be sentenced. You have told me that you went to Leatherslade Farm knowing you were doing wrong, that you became involved, but not in the robbery, and then ran away. I do not find it possible to differentiate your case from that of most of the other accused. You will accordingly go to prison for concurrent terms of 25 years on the first count and 30 years on the second count.

Gordon Goody

Douglas Gordon Goody, you have been convicted on the first and second counts of this indictment. You have a bad record, notably with a conviction for grave violence at the early age of 18, and you qualify for preventive detention. Yet, in some respects, you present to this Court one of the saddest problems by which it is confronted in the trial. You have manifest gifts of personality and intelligence which might have carried you far had they been directed to honesty. I have not seen you in Court for the best part of three months without noticing signs that you are a man capable of inspiring the admiration of your fellow accused. In the Army you earned a very good character assessment and it is easy to imagine you becoming, in an entirely honourable role, a leader of your comrades, but you have become a dangerous menace to society.

The Crown have said that they do not consider this criminal enterprise was the product of any criminal master-mind. I do not know that I necessarily agree with the Crown in this respect. I strongly suspect that you played a major role, both in the conspiracy and in the actual robbery. Suspicion, however, is not good enough for me any more than it would be for a jury. It would be, therefore, quite wrong for me to cause my suspicions to lead to imposing upon you any heavier sentence than upon other accused and I shall not do so. You will go to prison for concurrent terms of 25 years on the first count and 30 years on the second.

Brian Field

Brian Arthur Field, you have been convicted upon count one and count twelve of conspiracy to rob the mail and of conspiracy to rob the mail and of conspiracy to obstruct the course of justice. Of the righteousness of both verdicts I personally entertain no doubt whatsoever. You had earned an excellent reputation beginning with little original advantages. By a combination of native ability of no mean kind and hard work you had attained a responsible position of a solicitor's managing clerk. Your strength of personality and superior intelligence enabled you, I strongly suspect, to attain a position of dominance in relation to your employer, John Wheater. I entertain no serious doubt that you are in some measure responsible for the disastrous position in which that wretched man now finds himself, but it is for your own misdeeds and for them alone, that you now have to be sentenced. They are serious enough in all conscience. You are one of the very few convicted persons in this trial of whom it can be said with any degree of certainly what it was that you were able to contribute to the furtherance of criminal ends. Whether it was in your mind or that of Leonard Field or that of some other entirely different person that there originated the idea of acquiring possession of Leatherslade Farm by subterfuge by saying it was wanted for purely honest purposes, I have no satisfactory means of knowing. Whether it was simply a remarkable coincidence that two out of the four bags found in Dorking Woods containing over £100,000 were your property or whether the fact is an indication of your further complicity in the main conspiracy again I have no means of knowing, though naturally I loyally give effect to your vindication by the jury on both the robbery and the receiving charges.

But that you played an essential role in the major conspiracy is clear. Out of that there naturally flowed the later conspiracy to obstruct justice. I have borne in mind your antecedents, as spoken by the police, the contents of the probation officer's report and all those matters urged upon me by your learned Counsel. You express regret for the position in which you now find yourself and that is understandable. The concurrent sentences of the Court upon you are that on the first count you will go to prison for 25 years and on the twelfth count you will go to prison for 5 years.

Leonard Field

Leonard Dennis Field, you have been convicted on the first and twelfth counts in this indictments. Although you have but one previous conviction, which I ignore, you are a dangerous man. Not only have you perjured yourself repeatedly in this trial to save your own skin but on

175

your own showing at one stage you perjured yourself in an endeavour to ruin the accused, Brian Field. I sentence you not for perjury, but I sentence you solely for conspiracy. How and when you entered the major conspiracy I do not know. Whether you joined it at the instigation of another again I do not know, but an overt act committed by you in pursuance of that conspiracy is established beyond doubt and very important it was.

I cannot agree with your learned Counsel that your part in acquiring possession of Leatherslade Farm may properly be described as a small contribution to the criminal enterprise. On the contrary, it was a vital contribution. Once having joined the major conspiracy, the lesser conspiracy to obstruct justice was a natural outcome. I bear in mind your antecedent history and all those matters urged upon me by your learned Counsel. Having done so I can see no valid grounds for differentiating your case from Brian Field. You will accordingly be sentenced to concurrent terms of 25 years on the first count and 5 years on the twelfth count.

John Wheater

John Denby Wheater, your case is in many respects the saddest and most difficult of all. You are 42 years old, a married man with heavy family responsibilities and of excellent character up until the present crime. You too served your country gallantly in the war and faithfully in peace. There is no evidence that you have contributed to your present disastrous position by profligate living of any kind. Indeed your standards appear to have been distinctly lower than those of your managing clerk. Yet you, as a solicitor of the Supreme Court, stand convicted under count 12 of conspiring with Leonard Field and your managing clerk to obstruct the course of justice. The jury have acquitted you on the first count and I naturally treat you as having had no knowledge until after the mail train robbery of the criminal purpose for which you had been instructed to secure possession of Leatherslade Farm. Your conviction on the twelfth count establishes, as I interpret the verdict, that at some time after the robbery that criminal purpose became clear to you, as indeed it must have done, and you could then have given the police vital information by identifying Leonard Field as your professional client. A decent citizen would have volunteered to do that very thing whatever his strictly legal obligations must be. Instead, you professed inability to do so. That profession the jury have found was false and I regret to have to say that

I have no doubt the verdict of the jury in that regard was right. At that time not a single one of the accused had been identified and, indeed, it was not until some days later that Mrs Rixon picked out Leonard Field. But for that no thanks are due to you. Instead of assisting justice you were obstructing it and that at a time when speed was obviously of vital concern to the forces of law and order. Furthermore, your deliberately obstructive actions clearly sprang from the conspiracy between you and the two Fields. It is in respect of that conspiracy that you must now be sentenced

Why you participated in it I do not know and you have not told me. You learned Counsel has been able merely to hazard a guess. Whether or not all the facts, if known, would speak in your favour or to your prejudice I have no means of telling and must not speculate, but I am disposed to accept the view that you allowed yourself to be overborne in some manner by your more masterful and able managing clerk. I cannot accept the submission that the fact that the maximum punishment for being an accessory after the fact to felony, with which you were originally charged, is 2 years' imprisonment, offers a sure guide to the proper sentence for this criminal conspiracy. Such conduct on the part of any citizen is gravely blameworthy. The criminality of it is gravitated when practiced by an officer of the Supreme Court and that fact must weigh heavily against you. On the other hand, I realise that the consequences of your conviction are disastrous both professionally and personally. Bearing in mind all relevant considerations I have come to the conclusion that you must go to prison for 3 years and you will be sentenced accordingly.

SOURCE NOTES

ASSI	Courts of Assize files at TNA
BPNA	British Postal Museum & Archive
BRB	British Railways Board
BT	Board of Trade
BTC	British Transport Commission
BTCP	British Transport Commission Police
CAB	Cabinet
CBI	Confederation of British Industry
DPP	Director of Public Prosecutions
CUL	Cambridge University Library
DOJ	Department of Justice
FBI	Federal Bureau of Investigation
FO	Foreign Office
FOI	Freedom of Information
HLRO	House of Lords Record Office
HMSO	Her Majesty's Stationery Office
HO	Home Office
LO	Law Officers
MEPO	Metropolitan Police
NA	National Archive (USA)
NLW	National Library of Wales
RISA	Russian Intelligence Service Archive
SIS	Secret Intelligence Service (MI6)
SRA	Solicitors Regulatory Authority
TNA	The National Archive (UK)
TUC	Trades Union Congress
UCL	University College London
WO	War Office

Source Notes

1: January – Ice Box Britain

1963 weather reports and statistics; National Meteorological Archive, London

The Gaitskell Papers; C275 and G211, University College London (UCL), Manuscript Room

The Common Market 1961/63 FO1109, The National Archives, Kew

The Papers of President Charles De Gaulle, Series AG (5 AG 1), Archives Nationales, Paris

Foreign Relations of the United States, 1961-1963, Volume III, Vietnam (January-August 1963); SACSA Briefing, Department of State, Lot 67 D 54, ORG-3 WG/VN Mtgs with other agencies, US National Archives, Washington DC

Department of State, Central Files, 951K.6211/1-763, US National Archives, Washington DC

National Security Files, Vietnam Country Series, 1/63, J. F. Kennedy Presidential Library & Museum, Boston MA

2: February – Please Please Me

The Harold Wilson Papers, Bodleian Library, Oxford

The Lord George-Brown Papers, Bodleian Library, Oxford

House of Commons Debates, Fifth Series (Hansard)

Iraq Defence Implications; CAB 148/16/4, The National Archives, Kew

Correspondence from British Consulate in Damascus, 1963/4; FO Series 1098, The National Archives, Kew

Brian Epstein et al; *The New Musical Express*, 5 January 1963–28 December 1963, British Library Newspaper Library, Colindale

3: March – End of the Line

The Papers of President Charles De Gaulle, Series AG (5 AG 1), Archives Nationales, Paris

Archive of the Federal Bureau of Investigation (FBI), Alcatraz Escapes, file 76-26295 and D-397500, Washington DC

Records of the US Department of Justice, Record Group 60; RG129 (records of the Bureau of Prisons), US National Archives, Washington DC

Beeching: Cabinet Memorandums, CAB 129/113-114; Cabinet Secretary's Notebook, CAB 195/22-23; Cabinet Conclusions, CAB 128/37, The National Archives, Kew

Institute of Civil Engineers Library, Paper 6064 presented to the ICE Council by Brigadier Thomas Lloyd DSO MC, November 1955

4: *April – Ban the Bomb*

Cabinet Papers on Blue Streak; CAB 128/34-35; CAB 128/102; CAB 129/123, National Archives, Kew

Cabinet Papers on Skybolt; CAB 128/36; CAB 195/7; CAB 195/19, National Archives, Kew

Cabinet Papers on Polaris; CAB 128/34; CAB 129/101; CAB 129/113, National Archives, Kew

5: *May – It's All in the Game*

Duke of Argyle v Duchess of Argyle, 1962 SC (HL) 88, National Archives, Kew

Duchess of Argyle v Duke of Argyle, 1967 CH 302, National Archives, Kew

6: *June – Scandal*

Boxing Illustrated Magazine, May/June 1963

The Ring Magazine (British Edition), June/July 1963

Boxing Monthly Magazine, July 1963

Boxing News Magazine, June/July 1963

World Sports Magazine, June 1963

Cabinet Papers; Resignation of John Profumo; CAB 21/5481, National Archives, Kew

Resignation of John Profumo; PREM 11/4368-69, National Archives, Kew

Resignation of John Profumo, PREM 11/4370, PREM 11/4372- 75, National Archives, Kew

7: July – The Unthinkable
Transmission of Biographical Letter re H St John Philby, prepared by the British Foreign Office in 1945 for the First Secretary of the US Embassy, London; State Department, File 111 20A/7 RG84, US National Archive, Washington DC

Donald Maclean, (codenames WAISE, SIROTA, ORPHAN, LYRIC, STUART, HOMER), File No 83791, RISI Archive, Yasenevo, Moscow

Kim Philby (codenames STANLEY, SYNOK, TOM, SOHNCHEN), File No 5581, RISA Archive, Yasenevo, Moscow

Kim Philby, KGB Memoir (My Silent War), attached to File No 5581, RISA Archive, Yasenevo, Moscow

Moors Murders; *The Times*, 22 October, 29 October, 3 December, 6 December, 7 December, 8 December 1965; 27 April, 13 June,18 October 1966; BBC TV News, 6 May 1966

8: August – I Have a Dream
The Great Train Robbery; DPP 2/3717, DPP 2/3718, DPP 2/3719, DPP 2/3723, National Archive, Kew

Martin Luther King; Records of US Information Agency, Record Group 306, US National Archive, Maryland

Martin Luther King; Case File No 63, CIV 2889, Civil Case files, US District Court for Southern District of New York

Nuclear Test Ban Treaty, DO 182/26; WES 37/43/4 part A, National Archives, Kew

Nuclear Test Ban Treaty, Treaties and other International Agreements Series 5433, General Records of the US Government, Record Group 11, US National Archive, Washington DC

9: September – Thunderball
Breaching of Copyright; McClory/Whittingham v Fleming (1961-M-989)

McClory/Whittingham v Fleming, Court Order of 3 December 1963; Ian Fleming, Deed of Assignment, 31 December 1963, High Courts of Justice, London

The Denning Report; Guidance for posts; FO 953/2111, National Archives, Kew

Brief for the Secretary of State on Denning Report; HO 325/15,
    National Archives, Kew
Lord Dilhorne's Examination of the Security Reports re Stephen Ward;
    LCO 2/8270, National Archives, Kew
Disposal of Profumo Inquiry Evidence; HO 342/85; PREM 16/1453,
    National Archives, Kew

10: October – It's My Party

Resignation of Harold Macmillan; PREM 11/4804, National Archives,
    Kew
Lord Home becomes Prime Minister; URN 54941, Canister 63/93,
    Film ID 1780.02, British Pathe News Archive
Beatlemania; *New Musical Express, Melody Maker, Merseybeat,*
    British Library Newspaper Library, Colindale

11: November – Conspiracy of One

Assassination of John F Kennedy; FBI Case Files: 62-109060; 109090;
    105-82555, National Archives & Records Center, Maryland
Assassination of President Diem of South Vietnam; Tape Recorded
    Memo dictated by President John F Kennedy on Monday
    4 November 1963, The Miller Center, University of Virginia

12: December – Capitol Asset:

The Cyprus Conflict, FO 371/168978-168992, National Archives, Kew
The Beatles; Billboard and Cashbox newspapers, New York Public
    Library, NY

BIBLIOGRAPHY

Alford, Mimi, *Once Upon A Secret*, Hutchinson, 2012

Andrew, Christopher, *Secret Service*, William Heinemann Ltd, 1985

Andrew, Christopher, *The Defence of the Realm: The Authorised History of MI5*, Allen Lane, 2009

Barrow, Tony, *John, Paul, George, Ringo & Me: The Real Beatles Story*, Andre Deutsch, 2005

Bentham, Jeremy, *Dr Who: The Early Years*, W. H. Allen, 1986

Brivati, Brian, *Hugh Gaitskell*, RCB Publishing, 1996

Brown, George, *In My Way*, Victor Gollancz, 1970

Butler, R.A., *The Art of the Possible*, Hamish Hamilton, 1971

Callaghan, James, *Time and Chance*, Collins, 1987

Charlton, Sir Bobby, *The Autobiography: My England Years*, Headline, 2008

Charlton, Sir Bobby, *The Autobiography: My Manchester United Years*, Headline, 2007

Cook, Andrew, *The Great Train Robbery: The Untold Story from the Closed Investigation Files*, The History Press, 2013

Cooper, Henry, *An Autobiography*, Cassell, 1972

Costello, John and Tsarev, Oleg, *Deadly Illusions*, Century, 1993

Crosland, Anthony, *The Future of Socialism*, Jonathan Cape, 1956

Dallek, Robert, *An Unfinished Life*, Little Brown, 2003

Davies, Hunter, *The Beatles*, Heinemann, 1968

Dorril, Stephen, *MI6: Fifty Years of Special Operations*, Fourth Estate, 2000

Epstein, Edward J., *The Assassination Chronicles*, Carroll and Graf, 1966

Ferguson, Niall, *Empire: How Britain Made the Modern World*, Penguin Allen Lane, 2003

Bibliography

Ford, Gerald and Stiles, John, *Portrait of the Assassin*, Simon and Schuster, 1965

Gaitskell, Hugh, *The Challenge of Co-existance*, Methuen, 1957

Garrison, Jim, *On the Trail of the Assassins*, Sheridan Square Press, 1988

Guttridge, Peter, *The Great Train Robbery*, National Archives, 2008

Haining, Peter, *Doctor Who: 25 Glorious Years*, W.H. Allen, 1988

Hauser, Thomas, *Muhammad Ali*, Simon & Schuster, 1991

Healey, Denis, *The Time of My Life*, Michael Joseph, 1989

Hennessy, Thomas and Thomas, Claire, *Spooks: The Unofficial History of MI5*, Amberley, 2009

Hersh, Seymour, *The Dark Side of Camelot*, Harper Collins, 1998

Horne, Alistair, *Macmillan: 1957–1986*, Macmillan, 1989

Howard, Anthony, *RAB: The Life of R. A. Butler*, Jonathan Cape, 1987

Isaacs, Jeremy and Downing, Taylor, *Cold War*, Bantam Press, 1998

Johnson, Lyndon B., *The Vantage Point*, Holt, Rinehart Winston, 1971

Keeler, Christine, *Scandal!*, Xanadu, 1989

Kennedy, Jacqueline, *Historic Conversations on Life with John F. Kennedy*, Hyperion, 2011

Kennedy, Ludovic, *The Trial of Stephen Ward*, Gollancz, 1964

King, Coretta Scott, *My Life with Martin Luther King Jr*, Holt Reinhart Winston, 1969

Lane, Mark, *Rush to Judgment*, Simon and Schuster, 1966

Lapping, Brian, *End of Empire*, Granada Press, 1985

Lennon, Cynthia, *John*, Hodder & Stoughton, 2005

Levy, Shawn, *Ready Steady Go*, Fourth Estate, 2002

Lewisohn, Mark, *The Complete Beatles*, Pyramid Books, 1993

Macmillan, Harold, *At the End of the Day*, Macmillan, 1973

Marchetti, Victor and Marks, John, *The CIA and the Cult of Intelligence*, Dell, 1974

Marr, Andrew, *The History of Modern Britain*, Macmillan, 2007

Marrs, Jim, *Crossfire*, Carroll and Graf, 1989

Matthews, Sir Stanley, *My Autobiography: The Way it Was*, Headline, 2000

Maudling, Reginald, *Memoirs*, Sidgwick & Jackson, 1978

McDermott, Geoffrey, *Leader Lost*, Leslie Freewin, 1972

Moore, Jim, *Conspiracy of One*, Summit Group, 1990

Norman, Phillip, *John Lennon: The Life*, Harper Collins, 2008

Bibliography

Parissien, Stephen, *Assassinated*, Quercus, 2008

Paterson, Peter, *Tired and Emotional: The Life of Lord George Brown*, Chatto & Windus, 1993

Pelling, Henry, *A Short History of the Labour Party*, Macmillan, (eighth edition) 1985

Pimlott, Ben, *Harold Wilson*, Harper Collins, 1992

Posner, Gerald, *Case Closed*, Random House, 1993

Read, Piers Paul, *The Train Robbers*, W.H. Allen, 1978

Remnick, David, *King of the World: Muhammad Ali & the Rise of the American Hero*, Picador, 1998

'Report of the President's Commission on the Assassination of President John F. Kennedy' (The Warren Commission), United States Government Printing Office, 1964

Reynolds, Bruce, *Crossing the Line: The Autobiography of a Thief*, Virgin, 2003

Sandbrook, Dominic, *Never Had It So Good*, Little, Brown, 2005

Schlesinger, Arthur, *A Thousand Days*, Houghton Mifflin & Co., 1965

Sellers, Robert, *The Battle for Bond*, Tomahawk Press, 2007

Shaffner, Nicholas and Shotton, Pete, *John Lennon: In My Life*, Coronet Books, 1984

Spizer, Bruce, *The Beatles' Story on Capitol Records (Part 1 & 2)*, 498 Publishing, 2000

Summers, Anthony, *Conspiracy*, Gollancz, 1980

The Beatles Anthology, Chronicle Book, 2000

Weisberg, Harold, *Case Open*, Carroll and Graf, 1994

West, Nigel and Tsarev, Oleg, *The Crown Jewels*, Harper Collins, 1998

Wheen, Francis, *The Sixties*, Channel 4, 1982

Williams, Phillip, *Hugh Gaitskell*, Jonathan Cape, 1979

Wilson, Harold, *Memoirs 1916–1964*, Weidenfeld Michael Joseph, 1986

Wilson, Harold, *The Relevance of British Socialism*, Weidenfeld and Nicolson, 1964

Wood, Anthony, *Great Britain 1900–1965*, Longman, 1978

Wright, Tony and Carter Matt, *The People's Party*, Thames and Hudson, 1997

INDEX

Entries in **bold** refer to the picture number in the plate section

Index